220 ESSE SIGHT WORDS

An Activity Workbook to Learn, Spell, Trace & Practice the Most Common High Frequency Words

This workbook belongs to:

_____

- -

_____

Created by
Julie S. Miller

>>>>>

SMARTDEV PRESS

Free Goodies

Hello, Parents!

If you would like to receive our

TOP 10
Sight Words Activities
(Pre-Primary, Primary, 1st, 2nd, 3rd Grade),

please send us an email with the text
"More Sight Words Worksheets"
at

contact@smartdevpress.com

SMARTDEV PRESS

About the Author

Julie S. Miller (aka "Juliet") is the content creator and illustrator behind SmartDev Press, the publishing company that she has founded together with her husband in July, 2022. After enjoying an extensive career in English and Chinese language teaching (and after realizing that motherhood is her main passion), Julie shifted her focus toward creating qualitative artwork that supports children language development. She spends her days creating content and illustrating, drawing, reading literature, and exploring her favorite city on Earth - Charleston, South Carolina. She loves good music, walks in nature, being an active member of the community, and living alongside her family: a wonderful husband and their precious 4-year-old son.

At SmartDev Press, as former full-time childcare educators, we are keen to spread positivity and awaken creativity through meaningful and highly-qualitative work.
We value compassion, honesty and respect and believe in people with potential and a desire to grow.

Feel free to explore our book collection, but only if you find this book right here useful.

Visit our website:
www.smartdevpress.com

And if you feel like there is something we have in common, let's connect:

Find us on Instagram:
@smartdevpress

Find us on Facebook:
@smartdevpress

Note to Parents and Caregivers

First of all, at SmartDev Press we regard parents (and caregivers) as the partners in their child(ren)'s learning and development. This belief comes from our experience as parents, as well as from proven child-centered educational theories. Another belief is that learning should be fun, while another one obliges us to come with resources that would REALLY help them through this beautiful journey that life is. This is just to make sure we get aligned on expectations.☆☆

Secondly, this workbook (Vol. 1) contains all the 220 Dolch Sight Words. We have organized them into 5 chapters according to the level of education children should have to memorize these words. Nevertheless, what some people do not know is that this collection (created by Dr. Edward William Dolch back in 1936) only holds the so-called "service words". Dolch later released another list of 95 nouns, which is the subject of our next Sight Words Workbook (Vol. 2). And in this way, now you know what the next workbook for your child(ren) will be. ☺

Getting back to our approach, we do believe in Dr. Edward William Dolch's logic according to which "these words can only be learned by sight". Yes, we do know the lists were compiled back in 1936 but although modern vocabulary is currently more abundant in terms of "service words", the 220 words in this workbook (still) account for 50% to 75% of all words used in school textbooks, library books, newspapers and magazines nowadays. And this could be just the reason why we need to praise Dr. Dolch once again for being the road opener English-speaking people needed.

Finally, we choose to go with Dolch's 220 sight words only, no matter the efforts other researchers (e.g. Fry) took over the years to decide upon words frequency rankings. Given the fact that Dolch was looking at words that children in grades K-2 would be reading, the present workbook addresses the needs of children aged 4-8. Nevertheless, as the exercises inside require a certain complexity and fine motor skills development (e.g. use one hand consistently for tracing and drawing; cut along a straight line with scissors etc.), we decided to go with the 5-7 age group so that we make sure the little users will feel joy, confidence and self-esteem after each completed task.

With these being said, let's make the most out of this educational resource!

With ,

Juliet

How to Use this Workbook

As you might have already realized, this workbook is not meant to be used for tracing only. In our eyes, that is not the only way to learn sight words, therefore we have included a multitude of activities. Our worksheets inside this workbook are designed to help kids move from very simple to complex topics in very small steps, with only a slight increase in difficulty. This allows them to gradually develop their skills as they learn at the appropriate level and progress almost effortlessly. This slow increase in difficulty increases the likelihood that kids will be able to solve assignments independently, thus improving their self-learning skills. Still, be aware that some sight words (e.g. "right") have different meanings and that only one of those was treated in this workbook (our pick).

In terms of writing tools to be used, there is no suggestion coming from us for the moment, but any pen, pencil, crayon or felt-tipped pen is recommended, as long as the tip isn't too sharp. In the same time, please make sure that bleeding through the paper due to writing tool used should be avoided.

The decision of including the phonetic transcription (found next to each of the **220** sight words inside it) is based on the necessity of knowing that (at times) there are differences in pronunciation between American English and British English, no matter the early age of our users.
Besides those, we believe that the formulations and symbols used are understandable enough, therefore we won't focus on giving unnecessary instructions.
Except this one thing... [Please stay with your child for the next 10 pages!]

Hello there!
I am Buddy and I will be your learning partner for the next five chapters.

Buddy

Let the fun begin!
First, please color me in the color(s) you like most.

START

5 Alphabet Facts for the Start

Starting with the beginning: Let's get to know (about) the ABC's first.

For centuries, humans have portrayed crabs as perseverant and resilient. Read below to see also how wise they are.

1 English alphabet consists of **26** letters.

α alpha

β beta

2 The word alphabet is a compound of the first two letters of the Greek alphabet: <u>alpha</u> & <u>beta</u>. Can you guess which is which?

3 Look at the sentence below:

The quick brown fox jumps over the lazy dog.

What do you notice?

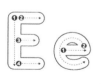

4 The most commonly used letter from the English alphabet is **E**.

5 The 26 letters of the English alphabet produce over **40** different sounds. Many letters have different pronunciations because there are more sounds than letters.

e.g. the C in "cold" sounds different than the C in "city".

7

Back to Fact #3.
Can it be that you noticed
that the sentence is displaying all the
26 alphabet letters?

3 Trace the **26** letters of the alphabet. How can you differentiate between small and capital letters?

♡ = Trace!

A A A A A A A   a a a a a a

B B B B B B   b b b b b b

C C C C C C   c c c c c c

D D D D D D   d d d d d d

E E E E E E   e e e e e e

F F F F F F   f f f f f f

G G G G G G   g g g g g g

H H H H H H   h h h h h h

I I I I I I   i i i i i i

J J J J J J   j j j j j j

KKKKK   kkkkk

LLLLL   lllll

MMMMM   mmmmm

NNNNN   nnnnn

OOOOO   ooooo

PPPPP   ppppp

QQQQQ   qqqqq

RRRRR   rrrrr

SSSSS   sssss

TTTTT   ttttt

20 so far.
6 to go...

◯ = Circle!

What is the first
letter of
the alphabet?
Circle the correct
answer.

A

B

9

Uuuuuu   Uuuuuu

Vvvvvv   Vvvvvv

Wwwww   Wwwww

Xxxxxx   Xxxxxx

Yyyyyy   Yyyyyy

Zzzzzz   Zzzzzz

= Write!

Can you write your name?

Please write it below.

WELL Done

Now let's learn the SIGHT WORDS!

10

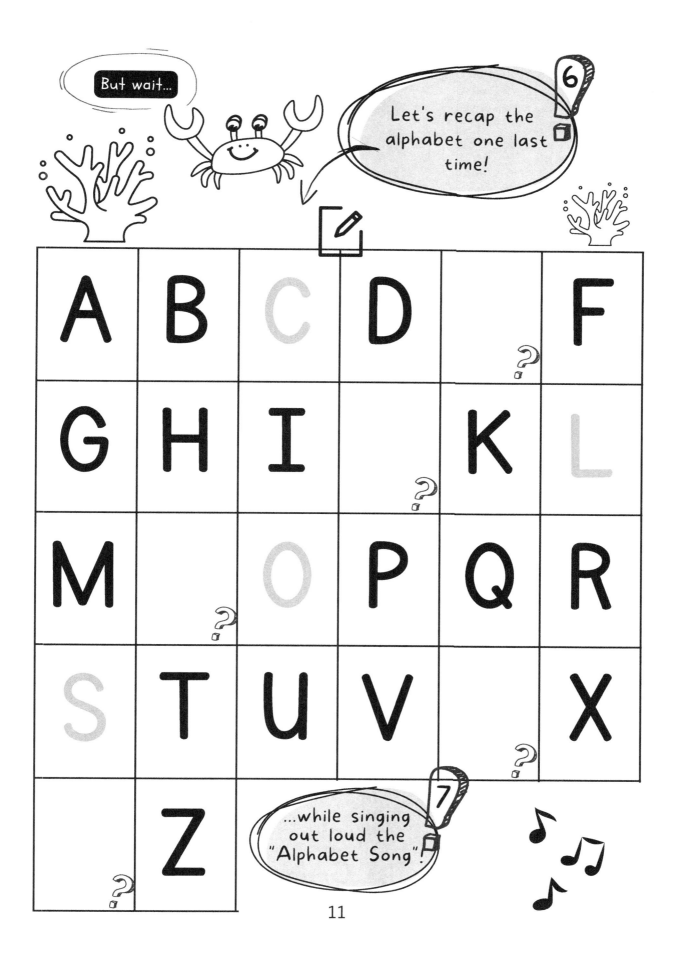

220 Dolch Sight Words List

"Service Words" –
by Corresponding Educational Level

1. a
2. and
3. away
4. big
5. blue
6. can
7. come
8. down
9. find
10. for
11. funny
12. go
13. help
14. here
15. in
16. is
17. it
18. jump
19. little
20. look
21. make
22. me
23. my
24. not
25. one
26. play
27. red
28. run
29. said
30. see
31. the
32. three
33. to
34. two
35. up
36. we
37. where
38. yellow
39. you
40. I

Pre-primer

41. all
42. am
43. are
44. at
45. ate
46. be
47. black
48. brown
49. but
50. came
51. did
52. do
53. eat
54. four
55. get
56. good
57. have
58. he
59. into
60. like
61. must
62. new
63. no
64. now
65. on
66. our
67. out
68. please
69. pretty
70. ran
71. ride
72. saw
73. say
74. she
75. so
76. soon
77. that
78. there
79. they
80. this
81. too
82. under
83. want
84. was
85. well
86. went
87. what
88. white
89. who
90. will
91. with
92. yes

Primer

93. after
94. again
95. an
96. any
97. as
98. ask
99. by
100. could
101. every
102. fly
103. from
104. give
105. going
106. had
107. has
108. her
109. him
110. his
111. how
112. just
113. know
114. let
115. live
116. may
117. of
118. old
119. once
120. open
121. over
122. put
123. round
124. some
125. stop
126. take
127. thank
128. them
129. then
130. think
131. walk
132. were
133. when

1st Grade

134. always
135. around
136. because
137. been
138. before
139. best
140. both
141. buy
142. call
143. cold
144. does
145. don't
146. fast
147. first
148. five
149. found
150. gave
151. goes
152. green
153. its
154. made
155. many
156. off
157. or
158. pull
159. read
160. right
161. sing
162. sit
163. sleep
164. tell
165. their
166. these
167. those
168. upon
169. us
170. use
171. very
172. wash
173. which
174. why
175. wish
176. work
177. would
178. write
179. your

180. about
181. better
182. bring
183. carry
184. clean
185. cut
186. done
187. draw
188. drink
189. eight
190. fall
191. far
192. full
193. got
194. grow
195. hold
196. hot
197. hurt
198. if
199. keep
200. kind
201. laugh
202. light
203. long
204. much
205. myself
206. never
207. only
208. own
209. pick
210. seven
211. shall
212. show
213. six
214. small
215. start
216. ten
217. today
218. together
219. try
220. warm

3rd Grade

2nd Grade

12

sight word - page

220 Dolch Sight Words List

"Service Words" - in Alphabetical Order

a - 15	done - 140	I - 51	out - 72	these - 128
about - 138	don't - 118	if - 145	over - 104	they - 81
after - 90	down - 24	in - 31	own - 150	think - 109
again - 90	draw - 141	into - 69	pick - 150	this - 81
all - 56	drink - 141	is - 32	play - 40	those - 129
always - 115	eat - 66	it - 33	please - 74	three - 46
am - 57	eight - 141	its - 123	pretty - 74	to - 47
an - 90	every - 93	jump - 33	pull - 125	today - 153
and - 17	fall - 142	just - 99	put - 105	together - 154
any - 91	far - 142	keep - 146	ran - 75	too - 82
are - 57	fast - 119	kind - 146	read - 125	try - 154
around - 115	find - 25	know - 100	red - 43	two - 47
as - 91	first - 119	laugh - 146	ride - 75	under - 82
ask - 91	five - 119	let - 100	right - 125	up - 48
at - 58	fly - 94	light - 147	round - 105	upon - 129
ate - 58	for - 26	like - 69	run - 44	us - 129
away - 18	found - 122	little - 34	said - 44	use - 130
be - 58	four - 66	live - 100	saw - 75	very - 130
because - 115	from - 94	long - 147	say - 78	walk - 110
been - 116	full - 142	look - 36	see - 45	want - 82
before - 116	funny - 29	made - 123	seven - 150	warm - 154
best - 116	gave - 122	make - 36	shall - 151	was - 83
better - 138	get - 66	many - 124	she - 78	wash - 130
big - 19	give - 95	may - 102	show - 151	we - 49
black - 60	go - 30	me - 37	sing - 127	well - 83
blue - 20	goes - 122	much - 147	sit - 127	went - 83
both - 117	going - 95	must - 69	six - 151	were - 110
bring - 138	good - 67	my - 38	sleep - 127	what - 85
brown - 60	got - 144	myself - 148	small - 152	when - 110
but - 62	green - 123	never - 148	so - 78	where - 49
buy - 117	grow - 144	new - 70	some - 105	which - 131
by - 92	had - 95	no - 70	soon - 79	white - 85
call - 117	has - 98	not - 38	start - 152	who - 85
came - 62	have - 67	now - 70	stop - 108	why - 131
can - 22	he - 67	of - 102	take - 108	will - 86
carry - 139	help - 30	off - 124	tell - 128	wish - 132
clean - 139	her - 98	old - 102	ten - 152	with - 86
cold - 118	here - 31	once - 104	thank - 108	work - 132
come - 23	him - 98	one - 40	that - 79	would - 132
could - 92	his - 99	one - 72	the - 46	write - 133
cut - 139	hold - 144	only - 148	their - 128	yellow - 50
did - 62	hot - 145	open - 104	them - 109	yes - 86
do - 63	how - 99	or - 124	then - 109	you - 50
does - 118	hurt - 145	our - 72	there - 79	your - 133

Table of Contents

1.
INTRODUCTION
pages 1-14

2.
PRE-PRIMARY SIGHT WORDS
pages 15-55

3.
PRIMARY SIGHT WORDS
pages 56-89

4.
FIRST GRADE SIGHT WORDS
pages 90-114

5.
SECOND GRADE SIGHT WORDS
pages 115-137

6.
THIRD GRADE SIGHT WORDS
pages 138-156

Now let's really start!

In a sentence:

I have a pet.

Sight Word #1. a

Trace the word.

a

Say it out loud.

a

US: weak /ə/ ; strong /eɪ/
UK: weak /ə/ ; strong /eɪ/

Trace the sentence. (Circle) the sight word "a". Draw the picture.

My pet is
a dog.

(Circle) the correct spelling of the word.

| ei | ai |
| a | an |

Color it.

a

Color in the correct number of syllables in the word.   ① ② ③

Read and trace the sentence. Then (circle) the sight word. you just learned.

I am a child.

You are awesooooome!

Trace the words for each object*.
Color the objects.

Sight Word

a butterfly

a boat

a cat

a cake

a duck

a dolphin

a flower

a frog

a guitar

*(on this page) by "object" we refer not only to objects, but also to insects, animals, plants etc.

16

In a sentence:

You and I should play now.

Trace the word.

and

Say it out loud.

and

US: strong /ænd/
weak /ənd/
weak /ən/

UK: strong /ænd/
weak /ənd/
weak /ən/

Trace the sentence. Circle the sight word "and".

Tom and John came.

Color in your favorite color(s) all the eggs containing the sight word "and".

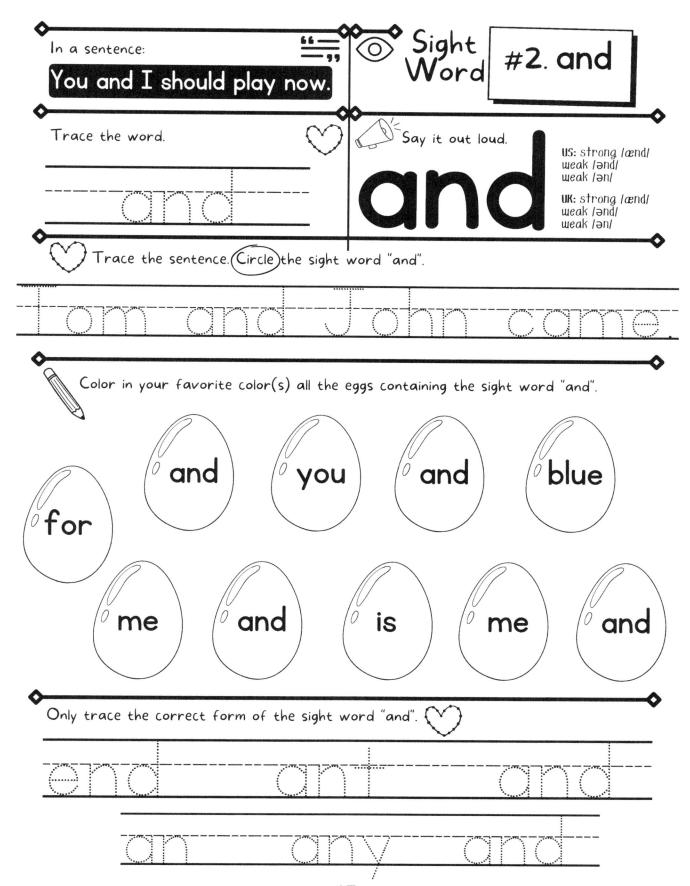

and   you   and   blue

for

me   and   is   me   and

Only trace the correct form of the sight word "and".

end   ant   and

an   any   and

17

Trace the word.

away
AWAY

Capital letters are generally more in height than the small letters.

Say it out loud.

US / UK: /əˈweɪ/

away

1
2
3
4 letters in total, right?

Color in the correct number of syllables in the word.

1 2 3

Match the jumbled words with the corresponding words learned so far.

edn   and

adn   away

yawa   end

Find the sight word.
It is written twice.

n	s	h	a	e
e	a	a	a	a
i	g	a	w	w
a	v	d	a	d
a	w	a	y	t

Write the word in a sentence below.

18

Color the letters of the word "big". Color the big hippopotamus.

a **b** c d e
f **i** h **g** j

small big

Say it out loud.

big
US / UK: /bɪg/

Meaning in English: large in size or amount (adjective).

Circle the correct spelling of the word.

bigg   bieg

beg   big

Think about something that is big. Write it down.

- - - - - - - -

Color in the correct number of syllables in the word.   1 2 3

Read and trace the sentence. Then circle the sight word. ♡

She has a big

♡

What could the meaning of this sentence be?

Ask someone close. What did you find out?

- - - - - - -

- - - - - - -

19

In a sentence:

Her eyes are blue.

Trace the word.

blue

Say it out loud.

blue

US / UK: /bluː/

Meaning in English: color (adjective).

Color in blue all the clouds containing the sight word "blue".

Read and trace the sentence. Then circle the sight word.

The sky is blue.

Trace the words for each object*.
Color the objects.

Sight Word

#5. blue

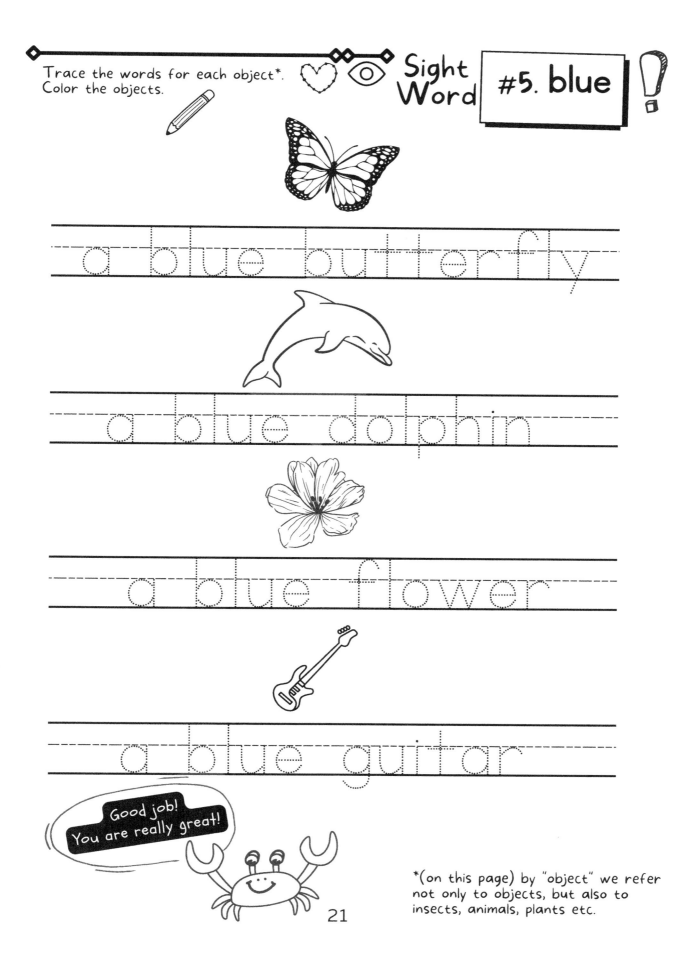

a blue butterfly

a blue dolphin

a blue flower

a blue guitar

Good job! You are really great!

21

*(on this page) by "object" we refer not only to objects, but also to insects, animals, plants etc.

In a sentence:

She can swim.

Trace the word.

------- can -------

Say it out loud.

US / UK: strong /kæn/ weak /kən/

can

Meaning in English: to be able to (modal verb).

Circle the correct spelling of the word.

chen

can't

can

cann

Color it.

can

Color in the correct number of syllables in the word.   1   2   3

can

What about this can?

What is it?

Set a goal for yourself. Think about it. Once you have all the information needed, tell it to yourself:

I CAN & I WILL

Ask someone close. What did you find out?

--- --- --- --- --- ---

--- --- --- --- ---

In a sentence:

He will come back.

Trace the word.

come

Say it out loud.

US / UK: /kʌm/

come

Meaning in English: to move or travel towards the speaker or with the speaker (verb).

Color it (x4).

come come

come **come**

Cut the letters and paste the correct spelling above.

o	m	c	e

Circle the down arrow.

📢 Say it out loud.

US / UK: /daʊn/

down

📖 Meaning in English: in or towards a low or lower position, from a higher one (adverb).

💡 Fill out the table below.

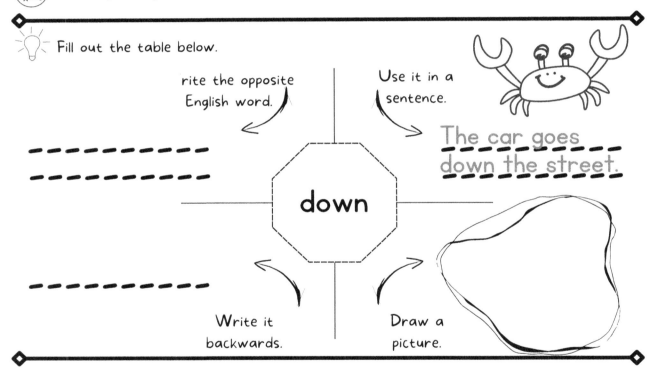

rite the opposite English word.

Use it in a sentence.

The car goes down the street.

down

Write it backwards.

Draw a picture.

✂ See previous page. ✂

You are awesooooome !

24

In a sentence:

I couldn't find you.

Trace the word.

find

Say it out loud.

US / UK: /faɪnd/

find

Meaning in English: to locate or uncover something that was missing (verb).

Color it (x3).

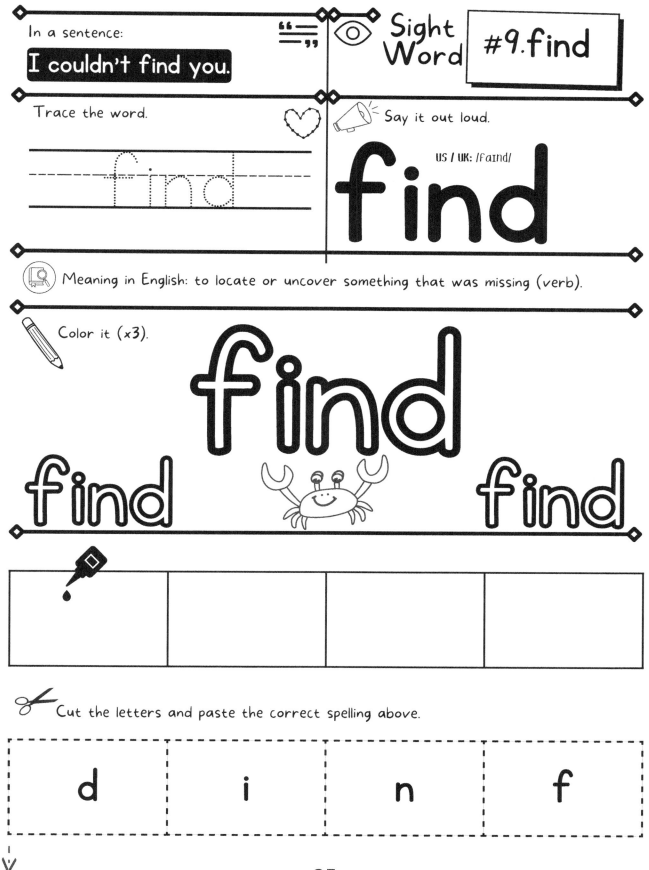

find   find   find

Cut the letters and paste the correct spelling above.

d	i	n	f

In a sentence:

This gift is for her.

Keep in mind.

FOR ≠ 4

Say it out loud.

for

US:
strong /fɔːr/
weak /fər/

UK:
strong /fɔː/
weak /fə/

Meaning in English: intended to be given to (preposition).

Match the jumbled words with the corresponding words learned so far.

cna   for

fuor   four

rof   can

waay   away

omec   come

Color the letters of the word "for".

(a)   (b)   (c)

(f)   (o)   (r)   (e)

Find the sight word. It is written twice.

n	s	h	a	e
e	f	o	r	a
f	g	a	c	w
a	o	d	a	d
a	w	r	y	t

See previous page.

26

Look at the word, cover the word, write the word from memory.

a	a	a	a
and			
away			
big		big	
blue			
can			
come			
down			
find			
for			for
...			away

27

◆ Roll a dice and practice your sight words in the boxes below.

⚀	⚁	⚂	⚃	⚄	⚅
down	for	and	come	can	find

🔍 Find your sight words in the find-a-word below. Tick them off as you find them.

d	o	w	n	b
a	w	a	y	l
f	i	n	d	u
o	c	o	m	e
r	a	g	i	b

away   find ✓

for 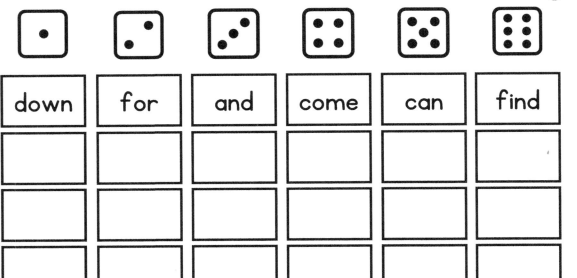 big

a   down

come   blue ✓

Read and trace the sentence.

‚ten sight words.

In a sentence:

Mike is so funny.

Trace the word.

funny

Say it out loud.

US / UK: /ˈfʌn.i/

funny

Meaning in English: humorous; causing laughter (adjective).

Look at the picture below. Arrange and write the words to make a sentence.

| The | funny. | boy | is |

Trace the word once again.

FUNNY

Draw something else that you think is funny.

In a sentence:

I will go to school soon.

Sight Word #12. go

Trace the word.

go

Say it out loud.

go

US / UK: /goʊ/

Meaning in English: to travel or move to another place (verb).

Color the letters of the word "go".

f   h
f   g   o   r

In a sentence:

How can I help you?

Sight Word #13. help

Trace the word.

help

Say it out loud.

help

US / UK: /help/

Meaning in English: to make it possible or easier for someone to do something (verb).

Color the letters of the word "help".

f   e   p   r
h   l   r

Color the two words.

go   help

#14. here

In a sentence:

I have lived here since 2018.

Trace the word.

here

Say it out loud.

US: /hɪr/
UK: /hɪər/

here

Meaning in English: in, at, or to this place (adverb).

Color the letters of the word "here".

a   c   e   e
  b   h   r

#15. in

In a sentence:

Molly is still in bed.

Trace the word.

in

Say it out loud.

US / UK: /ɪn/

in

Meaning in English: inside something (preposition).

Color the letters of the word "in".

f   e   n   r
  i   l   q

Color the two words.

here   in

31

In a sentence:

Mary is happy today.

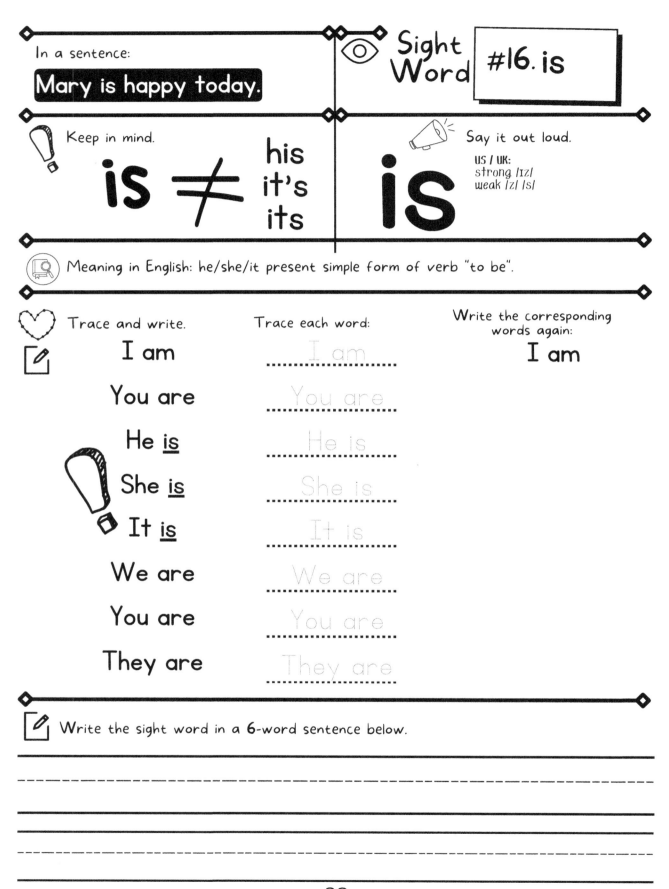

Sight Word #16. is

Keep in mind.

is ≠ his it's its

Say it out loud.

is

US / UK:
strong /ɪz/
weak /z/ /s/

Meaning in English: he/she/it present simple form of verb "to be".

Trace and write.

I am

You are

He <u>is</u>

She <u>is</u>

It <u>is</u>

We are

You are

They are

Trace each word:

I am

You are

He is

She is

It is

We are

You are

They are

Write the corresponding words again:

I am

Write the sight word in a 6-word sentence below.

Sight Word | #17. it

In a sentence:

It is raining outside.

Trace the word.

Say it out loud.

it US & UK: /ɪt/

Meaning in English: pronoun (third person singular); used as a subject of a verb.

Color the letters of the word "it".

(i) (t) (e) (e)
(b) (b) (r)

Sight Word | #18. jump

In a sentence:

I like to jump every day.

Trace the word.

jump

Say it out loud.

jump US / UK: /dʒʌmp/

Meaning in English: to push yourself suddenly off the ground and into the air using your legs (verb).

Color the letters of the word "jump".

(z) (j) (m) (r)
(y) (u) (p)

Color the two words.

it

jump

Color the letters of the word "little".

w   x   y
f   l   t   l   e
f   i   t   g   j

This is how you show "little" using your hands.

Say it out loud.

US: /ˈlɪt̬.əl/
UK: /ˈlɪt.əl/

little

Meaning in English: small in size or amount (adjective).

Use each sight word in a sentence.

big

little

Draw something that comes into your mind when you hear the word "little".

Cool!

34

Help the little kangaroo reach his mom.
Color the little one.

Sight Word | #19. little

Trace the words below.
Circle the sight words that you have learned so far.

the little kangaroo

the kangaroo jumps

k is for kangaroo

Let's find them!

#20. look

In a sentence:

We look out the window.

Trace the word.

look

Say it out loud.

US & UK: /lʊk/

look

Meaning in English: to direct your eyes in order to see (verb).

Color the letters of the word "look".

l   o   o   k
  c   h   r

#21. make

In a sentence:

I make my own clothes.

Trace the word.

make

Say it out loud.

US / UK: /meɪk/

make

Meaning in English: to produce or create something (verb).

Color the letters of the word "make".

z   j   r   e
  m   a   k

Color the two words.

look   make

36

In a sentence:

She likes me.

Trace the word.

------

me

Say it out loud.

US / UK: /miː/ /mi/

me

Meaning in English: used to refer to the person speaking or writing (pronoun).

Color in blue all the clouds containing the sight word "me".

Read and trace the sentence. Then circle the sight word "me".

She waved at me.

In a sentence:

He is my brother.

Sight Word #23. my

Trace the word.

my

Say it out loud.

US / UK: /maɪ/

my

Meaning in English: of or belonging to me (determiner).

Color the letters of the word "my".

x   z   m   k
  w   h   y

In a sentence:

You are not alone.

Sight Word #24. not

Trace the word.

not

Say it out loud.

US: /nɑːt/
UK: /nɒt/

not

Meaning in English: used to form a negative phrase (adverb).

Color the letters of the word "not".

n   j   r   t
  m   o   k

Color the two words.

my   not

38

Trace the words for each object*.
Color the objects.

Sight Word #23. my

my book

my donut

my drum

my hand

my heart

my iguana

my journal

my key

my laptop

*(on this page) by "object" we refer not only to objects, but also to insects, animals, plants etc.

39

Sight Word #25. one

In a sentence:

"Two" is larger than "one".

Trace the word.

one

Say it out loud.

US / UK: /wʌn/

one

Meaning in English: number, determiner.

I

Color the letters of the word "one".

u n m k
o e y

Sight Word #26. play

In a sentence:

Let's play together!

Trace the word.

play

Say it out loud.

US / UK: /pleɪ/

play

Meaning in English: to take part in a game or other organized activity (verb).

Color the letters of the word "play".

o p l y
b o a

Color the two words.

one   play

40

Look at the word, cover the word, write the word from memory.

funny			
help			
here			
is			
jump			
…		little	
look			
make			
me			
my			
play			

Pre-primer 2

Color the correct number of objects.

3

1

2

one

5

one

Count the numbers as you connect the dots. Then trace the sight words.

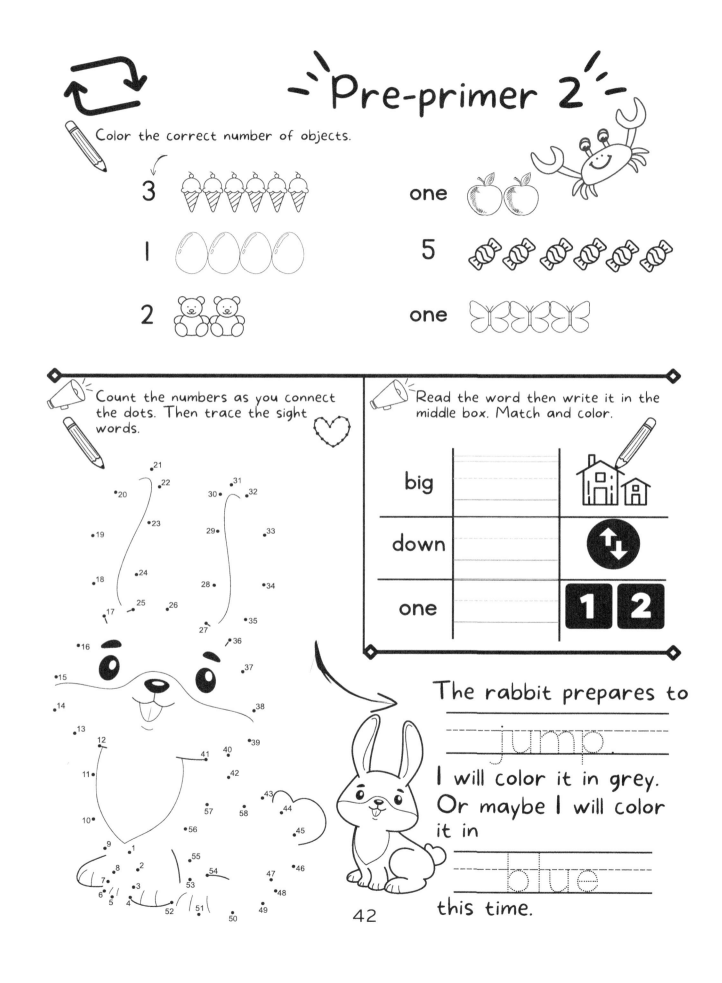

Read the word then write it in the middle box. Match and color.

big		
down		
one		

The rabbit prepares to

jump.

I will color it in grey. Or maybe I will color it in

blue

this time.

In a sentence:

She wears a red dress.

Trace the word.

red

Say it out loud.

US / UK: /red/

red

Meaning in English: color (adjective).

Color in red all the eggs containing the sight word "red".

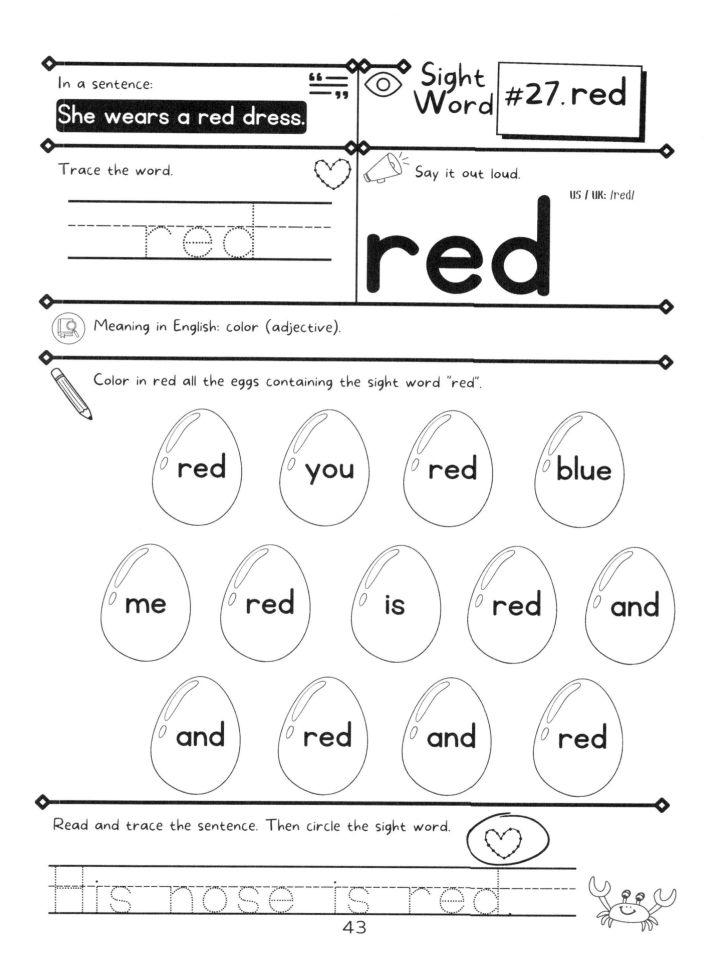

red   you   red   blue

me   red   is   red   and

and   red   and   red

Read and trace the sentence. Then circle the sight word.

His nose is red.

In a sentence:

She can run very fast.

Trace the word.

run

Say it out loud.

US / UK: /rʌn/

run

Meaning in English: to move along, faster than walking (verb).

Color the letters of the word "run".

r n m k
  u e z

In a sentence:

Danny said a funny joke.

Trace the word.

said

Say it out loud.

US / UK: /sed/

said

Meaning in English: past simple and past participle of verb "(to) say".

Color the letters of the word "said".

o p a d
  b s i

Color the two words.

run   said

44

Sight Word **#30. see**

In a sentence:

See you later, Mike!

Trace the word.

s e e

Say it out loud.

US / UK: /siː/

see

Meaning in English: to use your eyes for knowing what is around (verb).

Circle the correct spelling of the word.

si	sea
c	see

Color it.

see

Color in the correct number of syllables in the word.

1 2 3

Look at the picture below. Arrange and write the words to make a sentence.

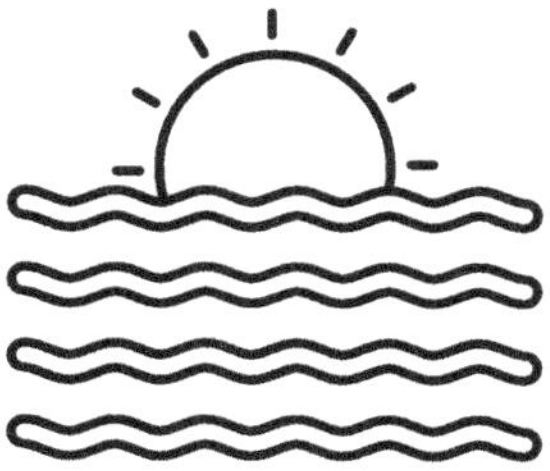

can | sea. | I | see | the

Trace the word once again.

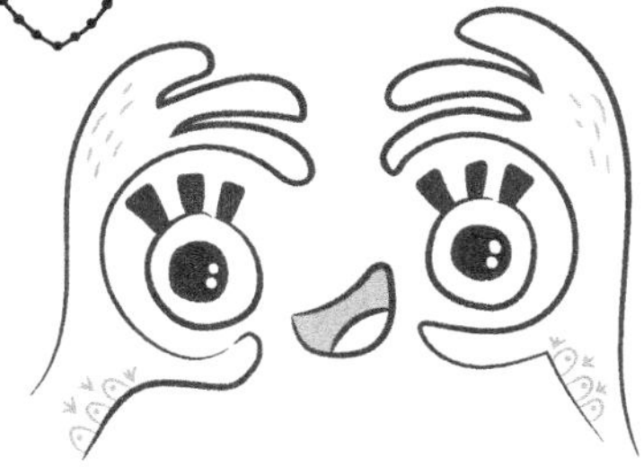

SEE

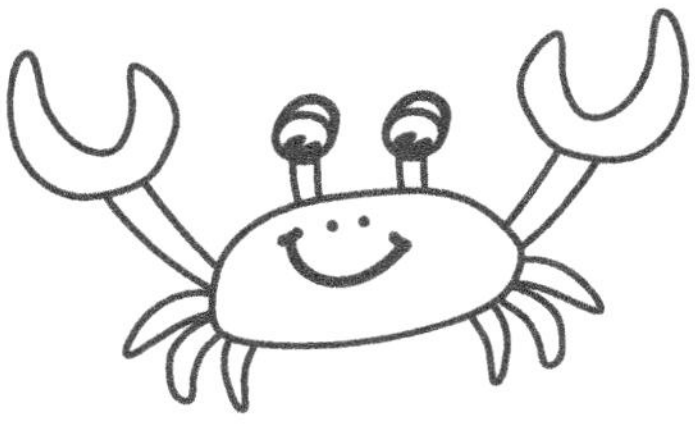

In a sentence:

We went to the beach.

Trace the word.

the

Say it out loud.

the

US / UK:
strong /ði:/
weak /ðə/

Meaning in English: normally used before nouns (determiner).

Color the letters of the word "the".

a   c   h   k
   o   t   e

In a sentence:

I have three best friends.

Trace the word.

three

Say it out loud.

three

US / UK: /θri:/

Meaning in English: number.

3

Color the letters of the word "three".

o   h   e   y
   t   r   e

Color the two words.

the   three

In a sentence:

I need to sleep now.

Trace the word.

to

Meaning in English: normally used before verbs (preposition).

Say it out loud.

to

US / UK: strong /tuː/
weak /tə/

Color the letters of the word "to".

a z h k
a t o

In a sentence:

My neighbor has two dogs.

Trace the word.

two

Meaning in English: number.

2

Say it out loud.

two

US / UK: /tuː/

Color the letters of the word "two".

r h e o
t w e

Color the two words.

to   two

Circle the "up" arrow.

📢 Say it out loud.

US / UK: /ʌp/

up

📖 Meaning in English: in or towards a high or higher position, from a lower one (adverb).

🧩 Match the jumbled words with the corresponding words learned so far.

✏️ Color the letters of the word "up".

f u o p

pu	said
idas	run
unr	up
reeth	three
rde	red

🔍 Find the sight word. It is written six times.

u	p	u	p	e
e	f	o	r	u
f	g	a	u	p
a	p	p	u	d
a	u	r	p	t

Circle the correct spelling of the word.

app	ap	uph	up

48

Sight Word #36. we

In a sentence:
We love this workbook.

Trace the word.

we

Say it out loud.

US / UK:
strong /wiː/
weak /wi/

we

Meaning in English: refers to a group including the speaker (pronoun).

Color the letters of the word "we".

a b c w h o e

Sight Word #37. where

In a sentence:
Where are we going now?

Trace the word.

where

Say it out loud.

US: /wer/
UK: /weər/

where

Meaning in English: to, at, or in what place (adverb, conjunction).

Color the letters of the word "where".

y w h e r e o

Color the two words.

we   where

49

Sight Word #38.yellow

In a sentence:

That is a yellow submarine.

Trace the word.

yellow

Say it out loud.

US: /ˈjel.oʊ/
UK: /ˈjel.əʊ/

yellow

Meaning in English: color (adjective).

Color the letters of the word "yellow".

a e l w
y l o

Sight Word #39. you

In a sentence:

Will you come with me?

Trace the word.

you

Say it out loud.

US / UK: /juː/ /jə/ /jʊ/

you

Meaning in English: used to refer to the person or people being spoken or written to (pronoun).

Color the letters of the word "you".

z h r u
w y o

Color the two words (I guess you know in which color, right?)

yellow   you

50

In a sentence:

I am fine, thank you.

Trace the word.

Say it out loud.

US / UK: /aɪ/

Meaning in English: the person speaking (pronoun).

Circle the correct spelling of the word.

Color it.

ai	i
I	eye

Color in the correct number of syllables in the word.

1 2 3

Look at the picture below. Arrange and write the words to make a sentence.

can | house. | I | see | a

Keep in mind.

I
NOT
i

"I" is the only personal pronoun that <u>must always be capitalized.</u> <u>This means we always use</u> <u>uppercase to write it.</u>

Look at the word, cover the word, write the word from memory.

you			
yellow			
where			
we			
two			
...		said	
run			
funny			
away			
little			
jump			

Color by sight word.

I = red
can = brown
you = yellow
up = orange
help = green
play = blue

Use each sight word in a sentence.

you

I

we

53

Identify the sight word, say it out loud, then write it next to the figure.

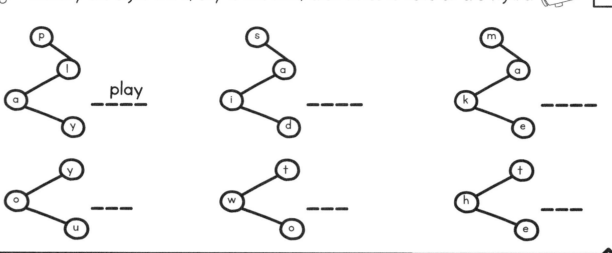

play ___

Think about the sight words that you learned and practiced so far.
Fill in the missing letter. Say the sight word out loud.

wh re

yel ow

thr e

litt e

j mp

mak

he e

fun y

pl y

ook

YOU are THE BEST!

Chapter Summary
Pre-primer

- There are __40__ pre-primer sight words;
- The two one-letter pre-primer sight words are _____ and _____;
- The three color words in this chapter are:

 | red | | | |

- Now I know how to write:

1 = __one__

2 = _____

3 = _____

- The **26th** sight word in this chapter is: _____;

- This is the _____ arrow;

- The **10th** sight word in this chapter is: _____;

- The two six-letter words in this chapter are _____ _____ ;

- In the remaining chapters I will learn and practice __180__ more words.

In a sentence:

All my friends love tennis.

Sight Word | #41. all

Trace the word.

a̶l̶l̶

Say it out loud.

all

US: /ɑːl/
UK: /ɔːl/

Meaning in English: every one of, the complete amount (determiner, predeterminer, pronoun).

Circle the correct spelling of the word.

owl | oll

hall | all

Color it.

all

Color in the correct number of syllables in the word.

1 | 2 | 3

Look at the picture below. Arrange and write the words to make a sentence.

| Have | drunk | really | you | all? | it |

MILK

_____

- - - - - - - - - - - - - - -

_____

Trace the two words using **6** different colors (3 for each).

ALL

Great job!

all

56

In a sentence:

I am hungry.

Trace the word.

am

Say it out loud.

US / UK:
strong /æm/
weak /əm/

am

Meaning in English: I present simple form of verb "to be".

I am

Color the letters of the word "am".

(a) (e) (l) (w)
(m) (l) (o)

In a sentence:

Are you hungry too?

Trace the word.

are

Say it out loud.

US:
strong /ɑːr/
weak /ɚ/

are

UK:
strong /ɑːr/
weak /ər/

Meaning in English: we/you/they present simple form of verb "to be".

They are   You are

Color the letters of the word "are".

(z) (h) (r) (e)
(y) (a) (o)

Color the two words.

am   are

In a sentence:

We'll meet you at the gate.

Trace the word.

Say it out loud.

at

US / UK:
strong /æt/
weak /ət/

Meaning in English: used to show an exact position or particular place (preposition).

In a sentence:

My sister ate all the cake.

Trace the word.

Say it out loud.

ate

US / UK: /et/ /eɪt/

Meaning in English: past simple form of verb "to eat".

In a sentence:

She will be here in a minute.

Trace the word.

Say it out loud.

be

US / UK:
strong /biː/
weak /bi/; /bɪ/

Meaning in English: used to show the possibility of something happening in the future (verb).

58

Find the five sight words. Circle them.

Sight Word #46. be

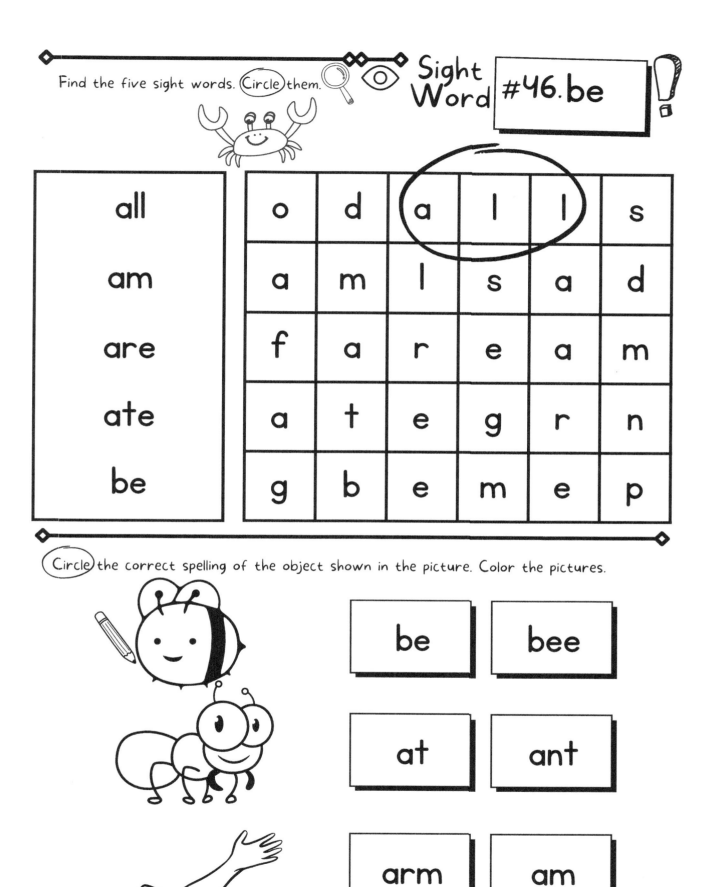

all		o	d	a	l	l	s
am		a	m	l	s	a	d
are		f	a	r	e	a	m
ate		a	t	e	g	r	n
be		g	b	e	m	e	p

Circle the correct spelling of the object shown in the picture. Color the pictures.

be	bee

at	ant

arm	am

Sight Word #47. black

In a sentence:

She wears a black dress.

Say it out loud.

US / UK: /blæk/

black

Trace the word.

black

Meaning in English: darkest color there is (adjective).

Color the letters of the word "black".

a b a k
m l c

Sight Word #48. brown

In a sentence:

He has brown eyes.

Say it out loud.

US / UK: /braʊn/

brown

Trace the word.

brown

Meaning in English: color of chocolate or soil (adjective).

Color the letters of the word "brown".

z r w e
b o n

Color the two words.

black   brown

Recap
Primer 1

Color by sight word.
Trace the sight words.

brown

black

blue   yellow   red

red   black   blue   brown   yellow

Use each sight word in a sentence.

am

are

at

ate

be

Sight Word #49. but

In a sentence:

I wish it rained, but it didn't.

Trace the word.

but

Say it out loud.

but

US / UK:
strong /bʌt/
weak /bət/

Meaning in English: used to introduce an added statement, usually something that is different from what you have said before (conjunction).

Sight Word #50. came

In a sentence:

He came home late.

Trace the word.

came

Say it out loud.

US / UK: /keɪm/

came

Meaning in English: past simple form of verb "to come".

Sight Word #51. did

In a sentence:

Did you do your homework?

Trace the word.

did

Say it out loud.

US / UK: /dɪd/

did

Meaning in English: past simple form of verb "to do".

Color the letters of the word "do". Then trace the word twice.

(z) (b) (c) (d) (e)
(f) (g) (h) (o) (j)

do do

Say it out loud.

US / UK: /də/ /du/ /duː/

do

Meaning in English: perform or take part in an action (verb).

Circle the correct spelling of the word.

| doo | thew |
| du | do |

Keep in mind.

Besides HAVE and BE, DO is one of three auxiliary verbs in English!

Color in the correct number of syllables in the word.

(1) (2) (3)

Read and trace the two sentences. Then circle the sight words learned so far.

Do your homework!

I did it already.

You are doing an amazing job!

Circle the right sight word to make the expressions correct. Trace the words.

do (make) **a noise**

do make a good job

do make a favor

do make an effort

do make a cake

do make the dishes

do make well

do make a journey

do make it yourself

Key: make a noise, do a good job, do a favor, make an effort, make a cake, do the dishes, do well, make a journey, do it yourself

Circle the right sight word to make the expressions correct. Trace the words.

Sight Word #52. do

(do) make — **exercise**

do make — money

do make — progress

do make — a promise

do make — the bed

do make — friends

do make — a guess

do make — an offer

do make — the room

Key: do exercise, make money, make progress, make a promise, make the bed, make friends, make a guess, make an offer, do the room

In a sentence:

What time do we eat?

Trace the word.

eat

Say it out loud.

US / UK: /iːt/

eat

Meaning in English: to put or take food into the mouth, chew it, and swallow it (verb).

In a sentence:

She has four brothers.

Trace the word.

four

Say it out loud.

US & UK: /fɔːr/

four

Meaning in English: number. 4

In a sentence:

She went to get some juice.

Trace the word.

get

Say it out loud.

US / UK: /get/

get

Meaning in English: to buy, obtain, or earn something (verb).

In a sentence:

Is it good or bad?

Sight Word **#56. good**

Trace the word.

Say it out loud.

US / UK: /gʊd/

good

Meaning in English: enjoyable, pleasant, satisfactory (adjective).

In a sentence:

I only have one brother.

Sight Word **#57. have**

Trace the word.

Say it out loud.

US / UK: strong /hæv/
weak /həv/ /əv/

have

Meaning in English: to own (verb).

In a sentence:

He is my best friend.

Sight Word **#58. he**

Trace the word.

Say it out loud.

US / UK: strong /hi:/
weak /hi/ /i/

he

Meaning in English: used to refer to a man or boy that has already been mentioned (pronoun).

Recap Primer 2

Identify the sight word, say it out loud, then write it next to the figure.

f, o, u, r ____

g, o, o, d ____

c, a, m, e ____

g, e, t ___

e, a, t ___

d, i, d ___

Think about the sight words that you learned and practiced so far.
Fill in the missing letter. Say the sight word out loud.

bla k

brow

fo r

ha e

go d

et

YOU ROCK!

Look at the picture below. Arrange and write the words to form a sentence.

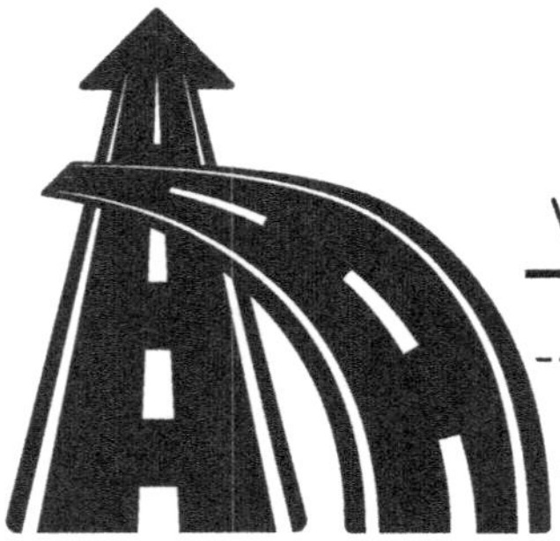

road	The	has	lanes.	four

In a sentence:

They went into the yard.

Trace the word.

into

Say it out loud.

into

US / UK: ˈɪn.tuː/

Meaning in English: to the inside of a place, area (preposition).

In a sentence:

I like her a lot.

Trace the word.

like

Say it out loud.

like

US / UK: /laɪk/

Meaning in English: to enjoy (verb).

In a sentence:

I am hungry, I must eat.

Trace the word.

must

Say it out loud.

US / UK: strong /mʌst/
weak /məst/ /məs/

must

Meaning in English: used to that something is necessary to happen (modal verb).

In a sentence:

I've just met my new pet.

Sight Word

#62. new

Trace the word.

new

Say it out loud.

US: /nuː/
UK: /njuː/

new

Meaning in English: recently started or created (adjective).

In a sentence:

Please tell me: Yes or no?

Sight Word

#63. no

Trace the word.

no

Say it out loud.

US: /noʊ/
UK: /nəʊ/

no

Meaning in English: used to give negative answers.

In a sentence:

I am not hungry now.

Sight Word

#64. now

Trace the word.

now

Say it out loud.

US & UK: /naʊ/

now

Meaning in English: at present time (adverb).

Trace the words and their opposites.
Then use each sight word in a sentence.

new   &   old

no   yes

now   then

new

no

now

Trace according to your answer to the question below.
Think about the fruits that you like. Which one is your favorite? Draw it.

Yes, I do

Do you like bananas?

No, I don't.

In a sentence:

He put his bag on the desk.

Sight Word

#65. on

Trace the word.

on

Say it out loud.

on

US: /ɑːn/
UK: /ɒn/

Meaning in English: above (preposition).

In a sentence:

Our team is the best.

Sight Word

#66. our

Trace the word.

our

Say it out loud.

our

US: /ˈaʊ.ɚ/ /aʊr/
UK: /aʊər/ /ɑːr/

Meaning in English: of or belonging to us (determiner).

In a sentence:

I suddenly got out of bed.

Sight Word

#67. out

Trace the word.

out

Say it out loud.

out

US & UK: /aʊt/

Meaning in English: away from inside (adverb, preposition).

Sight Word

#65. on

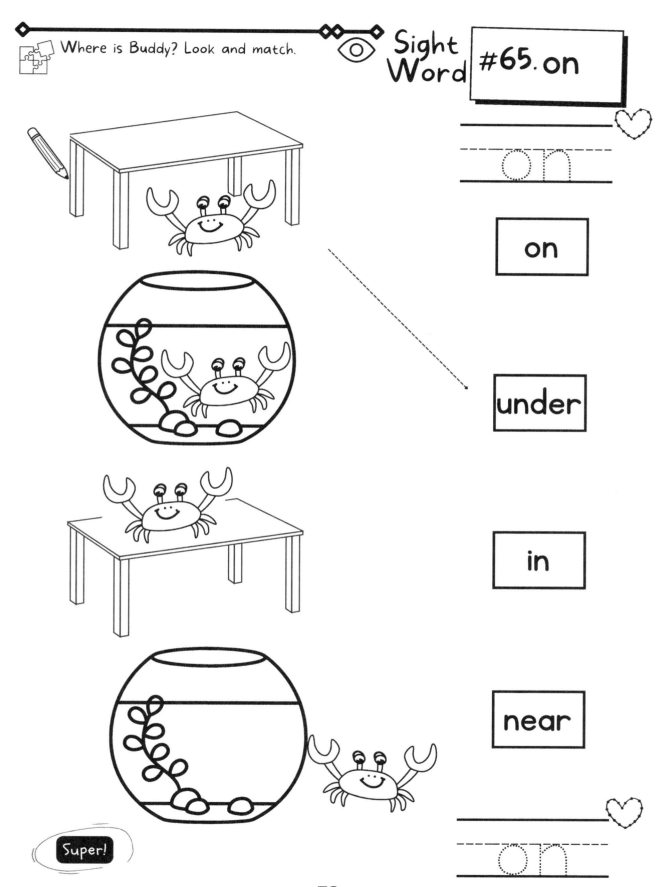

on

under

in

near

Super!

In a sentence:

Let's go out, please!

Trace the word.

please

Say it out loud.

US / UK: /pliːz/

please

Meaning in English: used to make a request more polite (exclamation).

Color the letters of the word "please".

a p l e e s a e

In a sentence:

I am pretty sure she ate.

Trace the word.

pretty

Say it out loud.

US / UK: /ˈprɪt̬.i/

pretty

Meaning in English: quite, but not extreme (adverb).

Color the letters of the word "pretty".

p b r e t t y

Color the two words.

please   pretty

In a sentence:

The dog ran after the cat.

#70. ran

Trace the word.

ran

Say it out loud.

US / UK: /ræn/

ran

Meaning in English: past simple form of verb "to run".

In a sentence:

Kevin can ride a bike.

Sight Word

#71. ride

Trace the word.

ride

Say it out loud.

US / UK: /raɪd/

ride

Meaning in English: to sit on something such as a bicycle and travel along (verb).

In a sentence:

I saw her dancing.

Sight Word

#72. saw

Trace the word.

saw

Say it out loud.

US: /sɑː/
UK: /sɔː/

saw

Meaning in English: past simple form of verb "to see".

Recap
Primer 2

Circle the word (or words) that rhyme(s) with the word inside the box.

see	**bee**	ankle	grandma
saw	cheek	so	jaw
ride	bike	bride	groom
ran	**fan**	**tan**	fish
now	ant	grandpa	cow
new	now	then	chew
our	hour	flower	your
out	throat	nose	doubt
must	dust	sand	rock
pretty	kitty	quite	gritty

Recap
Primer 2

Identify the sight word, say it out loud, then write it next to the figure.

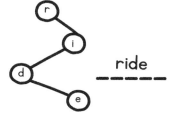 ride _ _ _ _ _

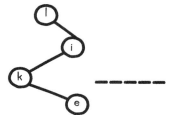 _ _ _ _ _

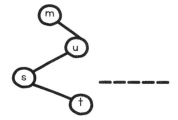 _ _ _ _ _

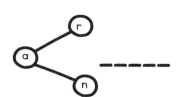 _ _ _ _ _

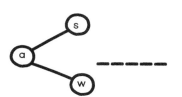 _ _ _ _ _

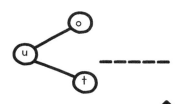 _ _ _ _ _

Think about the sight words that you learned and practiced so far.
Fill in the missing letter. Say the sight word out loud.

ple se

pret y

o r

o t

ne

goo

li e

m st

ave

f ur

GREAT WORK!

77

In a sentence:
She will say he is her hero.

Trace the word.

say

Say it out loud.

US / UK: /seɪ/

say

Meaning in English: to pronounce words or sounds, to express a thought (verb).

In a sentence:
I told you she will say so.

Trace the word.

she

Say it out loud.

US / UK: strong /ʃiː/
weak /ʃi/

she

Meaning in English: used to refer to a woman or girl that has been mentioned (pronoun).

In a sentence:
That horse is so beautiful!

Trace the word.

So

Say it out loud.

US: /soʊ/
UK: /səʊ/

so

Meaning in English: very (adverb).

In a sentence:

My friend will soon be here.

Sight Word

#76.soon

Trace the word.

soon

Say it out loud.

US / UK: /suːn/

soon

Meaning in English: in or within a short time; quickly (adverb).

In a sentence:

That boy runs very fast.

Sight Word

#77.that

Trace the word.

that

Say it out loud.

US / UK: /æt/

that

Meaning in English: used to refer to a person, object, idea, etc. (determiner).

In a sentence:

Put the box there, please!

Sight Word

#78.there

Trace the word.

there

Say it out loud.

US: /ðer/
UK: /ðeər/

there

Meaning in English: (to, at, or in) that place (adverb).

Color by sight word.

Sight Word #78.there

there = pink   she = green
that = red   say = blue
soon = orange   saw = purple
so = yellow   ride = black

look

There is a rainbow!

80

In a sentence:

They are very nice people.

Sight Word #79. they

Trace the word.

they

Say it out loud.

US / UK: /ðeɪ/

they

Meaning in English: used as the subject of a verb to refer to people, animals, or things already mentioned (pronoun).

Color the letters of the word "they".

t   b   a   y
  m   h   e

In a sentence:

This workbook is awesome!

Sight Word #80. this

Trace the word.

this

Say it out loud.

US / UK: /ðɪs/

this

Meaning in English: used for a person, object, idea, etc. to show which one is referred to (determiner).

Color the letters of the word "this".

z   r   i   s
  t   h   n

Color the two words.

they   this

81

In a sentence:

The room is too small.

Trace the word.

too

Say it out loud.

US / UK: /tuː/

too

Meaning in English: more than is needed or wanted; more than is suitable or enough (adverb).

In a sentence:

The ball is under the table.

Trace the word.

under

Say it out loud.

US: /ˈʌn.dɚ/
UK: /ˈʌn.dər/

under

Meaning in English: in or to a position below or lower than something else (preposition).

In a sentence:

I want to meet my hero.

Trace the word.

want

Say it out loud.

US: /wɑːnt/
UK: /wɒnt/

want

Meaning in English: to wish for a particular thing or plan of action (verb).

In a sentence:

I was sick last night.

Sight Word

#84. was

Trace the word.

was

Say it out loud.

US: /wɑːz/
UK: strong /wɒz/
weak /wəz/

was

Meaning in English: past simple form of verb "to be".

In a sentence:

She knows me very well.

Sight Word

#85. well

Trace the word.

well

Say it out loud.

US / UK: /wel/

well

Meaning in English: in a good way, to a high or satisfactory standard (adverb).

In a sentence:

I went to bed early enough.

Sight Word

#86. went

Trace the word.

went

Say it out loud.

US / UK: /went/

went

Meaning in English: past simple form of verb "to go".

Trace the present simple forms of the verbs and their past simple forms.
Then form sentences with the given verbs.

Sight Word #86.went

go	&	went
am		was
say		said

say

was

went

Circle the word or words that rhyme(s) with the word inside the box.

went	cent	sent	gift
go	many	low	so
goes	close	those	goose

In a sentence:

What time is it?

Trace the word.

what

Say it out loud.
US: /wɑːt/
UK: /wɒt/

what

Meaning in English: used to ask for information about people or things (determiner).

In a sentence:

I love white chocolate.

Trace the word.

white

Say it out loud.
US / UK: /waɪt/

white

Meaning in English: of a color like that of snow or milk (adjective).

In a sentence:

Who is she? A new friend?

Trace the word.

who

Say it out loud.
US / UK: /huː/

who

Meaning in English: used especially in questions as the subject or object of a verb (pronoun).

In a sentence:
I will stay at home today.

Sight Word #90.will

Trace the word.

will

Say it out loud. US / UK: /wɪl/

will

Meaning in English: used to talk about what is going to happen in the future (modal verb).

In a sentence:
Come with me, it will be fun.

Sight Word #91. with

Trace the word.

with

Say it out loud. US / UK: /wɪð/

with

Meaning in English: used to say that people or things are in a place together (preposition).

In a sentence:
Do you like me? - Yes, I do.

Sight Word #92.yes

Trace the word.

yes

Say it out loud.

US / UK: /jes/

yes

Meaning in English: used to express willingness or agreement (adverb).

86

Find and (circle) each sight word on the word search line.

1.	say	a r d s a y b e n u
2.	she	o f a r y g s h e y
3.	so	w w b a c k p o s o
4.	soon	m n o p s o o n q r
5.	that	c t h a t a r m n c
6.	there	b e d t t h e r e b
7.	they	t h e y w b e l l o
8.	this	h u n m t h i s i z
9.	too	w b i t o o d a y y
10.	under	u n d e r t o r t y

Look at the picture below. Arrange and write the words to form a sentence.

soon.	I	will	home	get

🔍 Find your sight words in the find-a-word below. Tick them off as you find them. ✓

w	a	n	t	h	w
e	h	c	t	a	e
n	t	i	s	i	l
t	i	a	t	l	l
w	w	t	i	e	z
o	w	w	h	o	x

want   white

was   who

well   will

went   with

💡 Look at the pictures below. Arrange and write the words to form sentences.

| time | it? | What | is | Nine? |

_____

- -

_____

| it | Yes, | nine | o'clock. | is |

_____

- -

_____

Chapter Summary
Primer

- There are _____ primer sight words;

- The two one-letter pre-primer sight words are _____ and _____;

- The three color words in this chapter are:

 black | | and | |

- Now I know how to write: → 4 = _____

END OF
CHAPTER 2

YOU'VE MADE IT ONCE AGAIN!
YOU ARE
EXTRAORDINARY!

- The 5th sight word in this chapter is: _____;

- I also know when to use "do" and "make". So, I

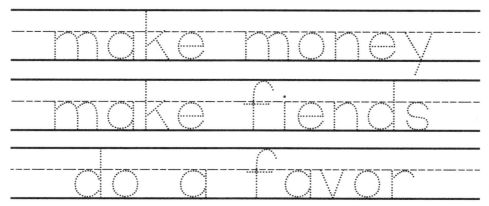
make money
make fiends
do a favor

WELL Done

89

In a sentence:

Her dog ran after mine.

Sight Word

#93. after

Trace the word.

Say it out loud.

US: /ˈæf.tɚ/
UK: /ˈɑːf.tər/

after

Meaning in English: following in time, place, or order (preposition).

In a sentence:

Will go again next week.

Sight Word

#94. again

Trace the word.

Say it out loud.

US: /əˈɡen/
UK: /əˈɡen/ /əˈɡeɪn/

again

Meaning in English: one more time (adverb).

In a sentence:

I eat an apple every day.

Sight Word

#95. an

Trace the word.

Say it out loud.

US / UK: strong /æn/ weak /ən/

an

Meaning in English: used instead of "a" when the next word begins with a vowel (determiner).

90

In a sentence:

Is there any cake left?

Sight Word #96. any

Trace the word.

any

Say it out loud.

US / UK: /ˈen.i/

any

Meaning in English: some, or even the smallest amount or number of (determiner, pronoun).

In a sentence:

They are as tall as I am.

Sight Word #97. as

Trace the word.

as

Say it out loud.

US / UK: strong /æz/ weak /əz/

as

Meaning in English: used in comparisons to refer to the degree of something (adverb).

In a sentence:

Can I ask you a question?

Sight Word #98. ask

Trace the word.

ask

Say it out loud.

US: /æsk/
UK: /ɑːsk/

ask

Meaning in English: to put a question to someone (verb).

In a sentence:

The car was driven by him.

Say it out loud.

US / UK: /baɪ/

by

Trace the word.

by

Meaning in English: used to show the person or thing that does something (preposition).

Color the letters of the word "by".

a b a e
p y s

In a sentence:

Could you help me, please?

Say it out loud.

US / UK: strong /kʊd/
weak /kəd/

could

Trace the word.

could

Meaning in English: used as a more polite form of "can" when asking for permission (modal verb).

Color the letters of the word "could".

p o u d
c e l

Color the two words.

by   could

In a sentence:

Every child has a hero.

Trace the word.

every

Say it out loud.

US / UK: /ˈev.ri/

every

Meaning in English: used when referring to all the members of a group (determiner).

Look at the superheroes below. Practice your drawing skills . Be creative!

Put your imagination to work!

Give names to the two superheroes!

93

In a sentence:

I wish I could fly.

Trace the word.

fly

Say it out loud.

fly

US / UK: /flaɪ/

Meaning in English: to move through the air (verb).

Color the letters of the word "fly".

f   b   r   y
   z   l   s

In a sentence:

He came back from school.

Trace the word.

from

Say it out loud.

US: /frɑːm/
UK: strong /frɒm/ weak /frəm/

from

Meaning in English: used to show the place where someone or something starts (preposition).

(A) - - - -
- - - - (B)

Color the letters of the word "from".

v   r   u   m
   f   e   o

Color the two words.

fly   from

In a sentence:

I give you this as a present.

Sight Word #104. give

Trace the word.

give

Say it out loud.

US / UK: /gɪv/

give

Meaning in English: to offer something to someone (verb).

In a sentence:

We are going home now.

Sight Word #105. going

Trace the word.

going

Say it out loud.

US / UK: /ˈgoʊ.ɪŋ/

going

Meaning in English: present continuous form of verb "to go".

In a sentence:

Last night I had a dream.

Sight Word #106. had

Trace the word.

had

Say it out loud.

US / UK:
strong /hæd/
weak /həd/ /
əd/

had

Meaning in English: past simple form of verb "to have".

95

Find and (circle) each sight word on the word search line.

1.	had	x r d b v h a d n u
2.	going	a m r u n g o i n g
3.	give	b v h g i v e x i u
4.	from	m f r o m o o n q r
5.	fly	q w e r t y f l y m
6.	every	l k j m e v e r y b
7.	could	p o y c o u l d v v
8.	by	b y h u n t y a r y
9.	after	a a a f t e r r r r
10.	again	a g a g a i n k y t

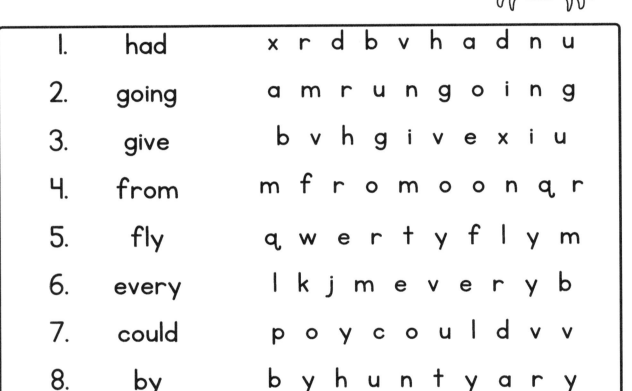

Look at the picture below. Arrange and write the words to form a sentence.

HELP!

| Could | please | you | me? | help |

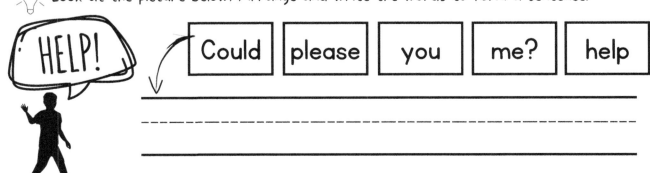

_____

_ _

_____

96

Color by sight word.

an = grey
ask = yellow
any = blue
fly = red
as = black

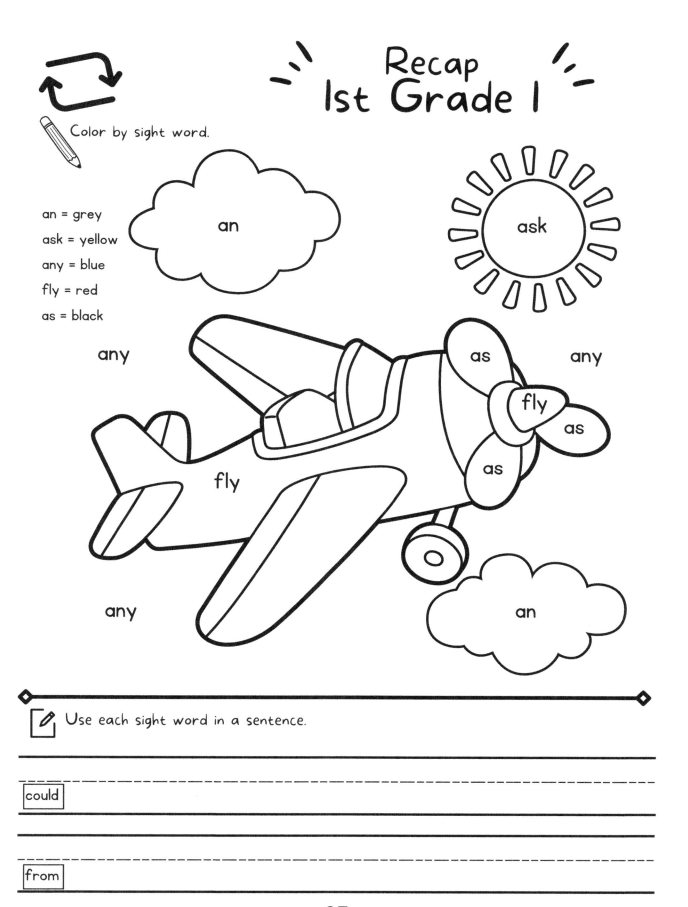

Use each sight word in a sentence.

could

from

In a sentence:

She has a bicycle.

Sight Word #107. has

Trace the word.

has

Say it out loud.
US / UK: strong /hæz/ weak /həz/ /əz/

has

Meaning in English: he/she/it present simple form of verb "to have".

In a sentence:

I gave her my favorite toy.

Sight Word #108. her

Trace the word.

her

Say it out loud.
US: /hɜːr/ /hər/ /ər/
UK: strong /hɜːr/ weak /hər/ /ər/

her

Meaning in English: used to refer to a woman, girl or female animal (pronoun).

In a sentence:

I gave him a small present.

Sight Word #109. him

Trace the word.

him

Say it out loud.
US / UK:
strong /hɪm/ weak /ɪm/

him

Meaning in English: used to refer to a man, boy or male animal (pronoun).

In a sentence:

What is his name?

Trace the word.

his

Say it out loud.

US / UK: strong /hɪz/ weak /ɪz/

his

Meaning in English: belonging to or connected with a man, boy, or male animal (determiner).

In a sentence:

How are you feeling now?

Trace the word.

how

Say it out loud.

US / UK: /haʊ/

how

Meaning in English: in what way, or by what methods (adverb).

In a sentence:

The driver has just arrived.

Trace the word.

just

Say it out loud.

US / UK: /dʒʌst/

just

Meaning in English: now, very soon, or very recently (adverb).

In a sentence:

I know that she loves me.

Trace the word.

know

Say it out loud.

US: /noʊ/
UK: /nəʊ/

know

Meaning in English: to have information in your mind (verb).

In a sentence:

He wouldn't let me cry.

Trace the word.

let

Say it out loud.

US / UK: /let/

let

Meaning in English: to allow something to happen or someone to do something (verb).

In a sentence:

People cannot live without water.

Trace the word.

live

Say it out loud.

US / UK: /lɪv/

live

Meaning in English: (to continue) to be alive or have life (verb).

Continue the pattern:

1. live let know <u>live</u> _____ _____ live

2. just how just _____ _____ how

3. his him her his _____ _____ _____

4. let her let _____ _____ her

5. has had live live _____ _____ _____

Keep in mind. Trace the verbs.

Verb TO LIVE – Present Simple
Affirmative Form

I You	~	live	in the USA.
He/She/It	~	live**s**	in the USA.
We You They	~	live	in the USA.

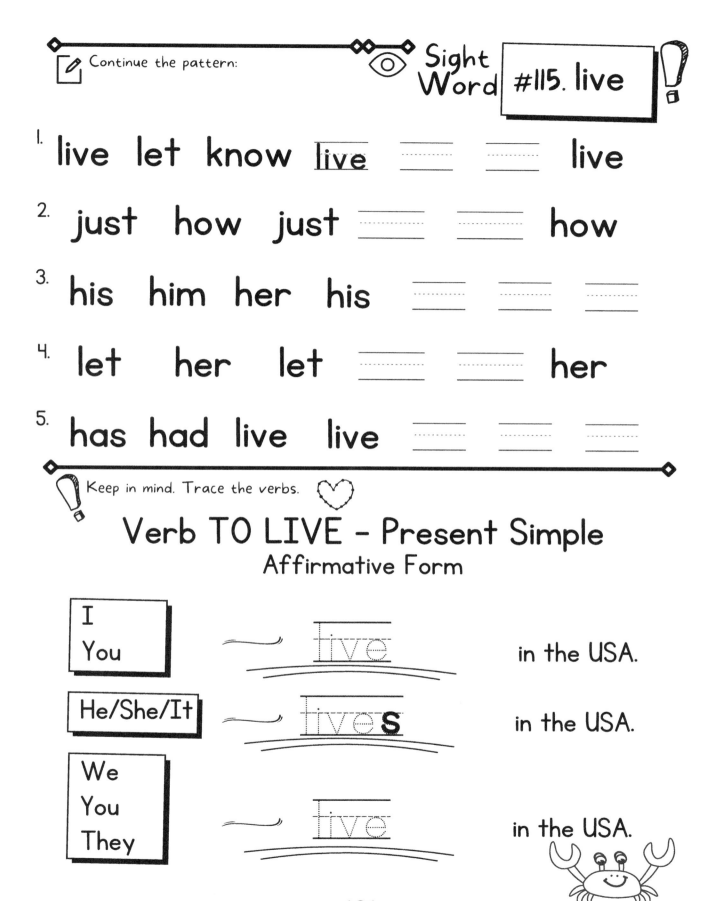

In a sentence:

I may see you tomorrow.

Trace the word.

may

Say it out loud.

US / UK: /meɪ/

may

Meaning in English: used to express possibility (modal verb).

In a sentence:

A friend of mine visited me.

Trace the word.

of

Say it out loud.

US: strong /ɒv/ /ɑːv/
weak /əv/

UK: strong /ɒv/
weak /əv/

of

Meaning in English: used to show possession, belonging, or origin (preposition).

In a sentence:

A wise old man taught me this.

Trace the word.

old

Say it out loud.

US: /oʊld/
UK: /əʊld/

old

Meaning in English: having lived or existed for many years (adjective).

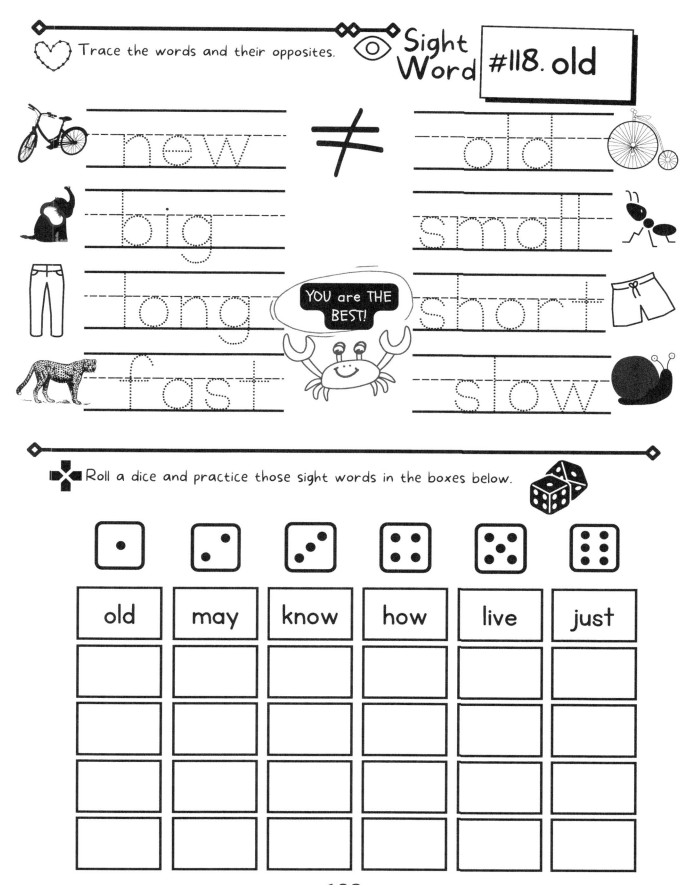

Trace the words and their opposites.

Sight Word #118. old

new ≠ old

big   small

long   YOU are THE   short
        BEST!

fast   slow

Roll a dice and practice those sight words in the boxes below.

old	may	know	how	live	just

103

In a sentence:

I've only talked to her once.

Trace the word.

Say it out loud.

US / UK: /wʌns/

once

Meaning in English: one single time (adverb).

In a sentence:

She left the door open.

Trace the word.

Say it out loud.

US: /ˈoʊ.pən/
UK: /ˈəʊ.pən/

open

Meaning in English: not closed (adjective).

In a sentence:

We went over a bridge.

Trace the word.

Say it out loud.

US: /ˈoʊ.vɚ/
UK: /ˈəʊ.vər/

over

Meaning in English: across from one side to the other (preposition).

In a sentence:

She put her bag on a chair.

Trace the word.

put

Say it out loud.

US / UK: /pʊt/

put

Meaning in English: to move something into the stated place, position, or direction (verb).

In a sentence:

Tennis balls are round.

Trace the word.

round

Say it out loud.

US / UK: /raʊnd/

round

Meaning in English: shaped like a ball or circle, or curved (adjective).

In a sentence:

There is some cake on the table.

Trace the word.

some

Say it out loud.

US / UK: strong /sʌm/ weak /səm/

some

Meaning in English: an amount of something that is not stated or not known (determiner).

Trace the sentences.

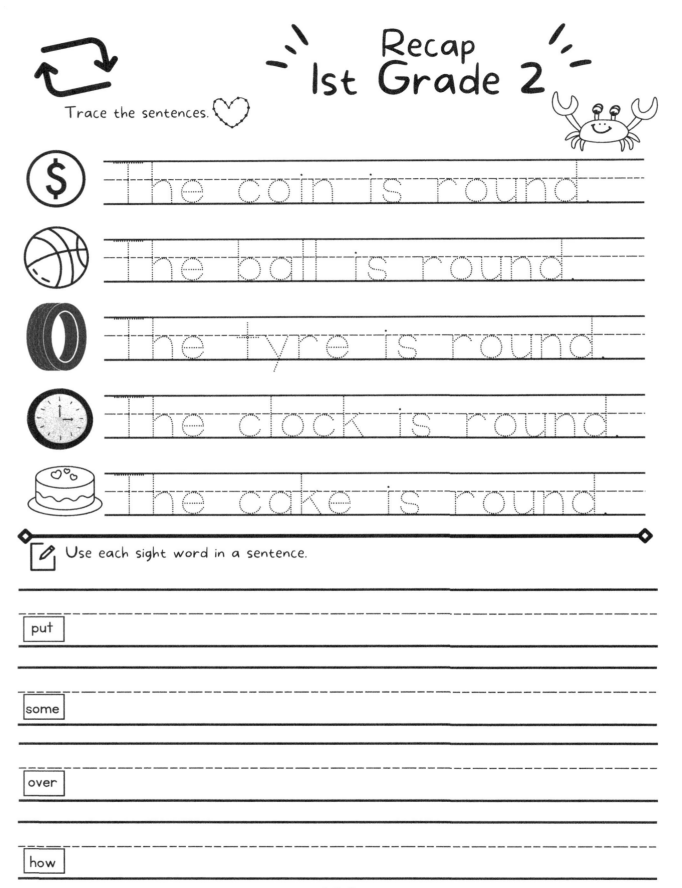

The coin is round.

The ball is round.

The tyre is round.

The clock is round.

The cake is round.

Use each sight word in a sentence.

put

some

over

how

Find your sight words in the find-a-word below. Tick them off as you find them. ✓

h	i	s	l	b
a	i	h	e	r
s	i	m	t	p
o	l	d	l	u
r	m	a	y	t

has   her

him   old

his   let

put   may

Circle the correct spelling of the sight words.

knou	nou	(know)	kow
live	laiv	livve	liv
oupen	oppen	opn	open
samm	soum	suum	some
giast	jast	just	juist

Sight Word #125. stop

In a sentence:

We will stop at the sign.

Trace the word.

stop

Say it out loud.

What color is the STOP sign? Color it

STOP

US: /staːp/
UK: /stɒp/

Meaning in English: to stay in a place (verb).

Sight Word #126. take

In a sentence:

I always take the bus.

Trace the word.

take

Say it out loud.

take

US / UK: /teɪk/

Meaning in English: to travel somewhere by using a form of transport or a vehicle (verb).

Sight Word #127. thank

In a sentence:

You can thank Emma for it.

Trace the word.

thank

Say it out loud.

thank

US / UK: /θæŋk/

Meaning in English: to express appreciation to someone for something he/she has done (verb).

In a sentence:

I can't see them anymore.

Trace the word.

them

Say it out loud.
US / UK: strong /ðem/ weak /ðəm/

them

Meaning in English: used to refer to people/things that have already been mentioned (pronoun).

In a sentence:

I was at the seaside then.

Trace the word.

then

Say it out loud.
US / UK: /ðen/

then

Meaning in English: (at) that time - in the past or in the future (adverb).

In a sentence:

I think that she likes me.

Trace the word.

think

Say it out loud.
US / UK: /θɪŋk/

think

Meaning in English: to believe something or have an opinion or idea (verb).

In a sentence:

I walk one mile every day.

Sight Word

#131.walk

Trace the word.

Say it out loud.

US: /wɑːk/
UK: /wɔːk/

walk

walk

Meaning in English: to move along by putting one foot in front of the other (verb).

In a sentence:

Where were you yesterday?

Sight Word

#132.were

Trace the word.

Say it out loud.

US: /wɜːr/ /wɚ/
UK: strong /wɜːr/ weak /wər/

were

were

Meaning in English: past simple form of verb "to be".

In a sentence:

Tell me when to call you, please!

Sight Word

#133.when

Trace the word.

Say it out loud.

US / UK: /wen/

when

when

Meaning in English: at what time; at the time at which (adverb, conjunction).

Look at the word, cover the word, write the word from memory.

when		put	
were		over	
walk		open	
think		once	
then		old	
them		of	
thank		may	
take		live	
stop		let	
some		know	
round		just	

Write the sight words in this chapter in alphabetical order.
You can write 4-5 on each line.

after again an any

Recap
1st Grade 3

✎ Use each given sight word in a sentence.

has

her

him

every

fly

an

may

of

old

Chapter Summary
1st Grade

- There are _____ 1st Grade sight words;
- The four one-letter sight words in this chapter are ____ , ____ , ____ , and ____ .
- There are ____ five-letter sight words in this chapter.

- Now I know how to write: know

CHAPTER 3

YOU'VE MADE IT ONCE AGAIN!
YOU ARE EXTRAORDINARY!

- The 8th sight word in this chapter is: _____;

- I also know what objects are round. For instance,

In a sentence:

It's always cold in this room.

US: /ˈɑːlweɪz/
UK: /ˈɔːlweɪz/

Form a sentence with the given sight word.

_____

- -

_____

Meaning in English: every time or all the time (adverb).

In a sentence:

They sat around the table.

US / UK: /əˈraʊnd/

Form a sentence with the given sight word.

_____

- -

_____

Meaning in English: in a position or direction surrounding (preposition, adverb).

In a sentence:

I like you because you are honest.

US: /bɪˈkʌz/ /bɪˈkɑːz/
UK: /bɪˈkəz/ /bɪˈkɒz/

Form a sentence with the given sight word.

_____

- -

_____

Meaning in English: for the reason that (conjunction).

always   around   because

Sight Word #137. been

US / UK: /biːn/ /bɪn/

In a sentence:

I've never been to Australia.

Form a sentence with the given sight word.

_____

- -

_____

Meaning in English: past participle of verb "to be".

Sight Word #138. before

US / UK: /rɪˈfɔːr/ /bɪˈfɔːr/

In a sentence:

He always gets up before 7 a.m.

Form a sentence with the given sight word.

_____

- -

_____

Meaning in English: at or during a time earlier (preposition, adverb).

Sight Word #139. best

US / UK: /best/

In a sentence:

This is the best birthday gift ever!

Form a sentence with the given sight word.

_____

- -

_____

Meaning in English: of the highest quality, or being the most suitable, pleasing (adjective).

been   before   best

116

In a sentence:

Both my brothers play soccer.

"—
—"

👁 Sight Word #140. both

US: /boʊθ/
UK: /bəʊθ/

💡 Form a sentence with the given sight word.

🔍 Meaning in English: (referring to) two people or things together (determiner, pronoun).

In a sentence:

I always buy books from there.

"—
—"

👁 Sight Word #141. buy

US / UK: /baɪ/

💡 Form a sentence with the given sight word.

🔍 Meaning in English: to get something by paying money for it (verb).

In a sentence:

She will call me when it's time.

"—
—"

👁 Sight Word #142. call

US: /kɑ:l/
UK: /kɔ:l/

💡 Form a sentence with the given sight word.

🔍 Meaning in English: to say something in a loud voice in order to get someone's attention (verb).

✏️ both   buy   call

In a sentence:

My hands are extremely cold.

Sight Word #143. cold

US: /koʊld/
UK: /kəʊld/

Form a sentence with the given sight word.

_____

- -

_____

Meaning in English: at a low temperature, (way) lower than body temperature (adjective).

In a sentence:

She does many after school activities.

Sight Word #144. does

US / UK: strong /dʌz/
weak /dəz/

Form a sentence with the given sight word.

_____

- -

_____

Meaning in English: he/she/it (present simple) form of verb "to do".

In a sentence:

I don't like it when you tease me.

Sight Word #145. don't

US: /doʊnt/
UK: /dəʊnt/

Form a sentence with the given sight word.

_____

- -

_____

Meaning in English: short form of "do not".

cold   does   don't

118

In a sentence:

She is a very fast swimmer.

Sight Word #146. fast

US: /fæst/
UK: /fɑːst/

Form a sentence with the given sight word.

_____

- -

_____

Meaning in English: moving or happening quickly, or able to move or happen quickly (adjective).

In a sentence:

This is my first visit to Arizona.

Sight Word #147. first

US: /ˈfɝːst/
UK: /ˈfɜːst/

Form a sentence with the given sight word.

_____

- -

_____

Meaning in English: coming before all others in order, time etc. (ordinal number, determiner).

In a sentence:

My father works five days a week.

Sight Word #148. five

US / UK: /faɪv/

Form a sentence with the given sight word.

_____

- -

_____

Meaning in English: the number 5.

fast   first   five

119

Write the sight word from the box that will make each sentence correct. ✓

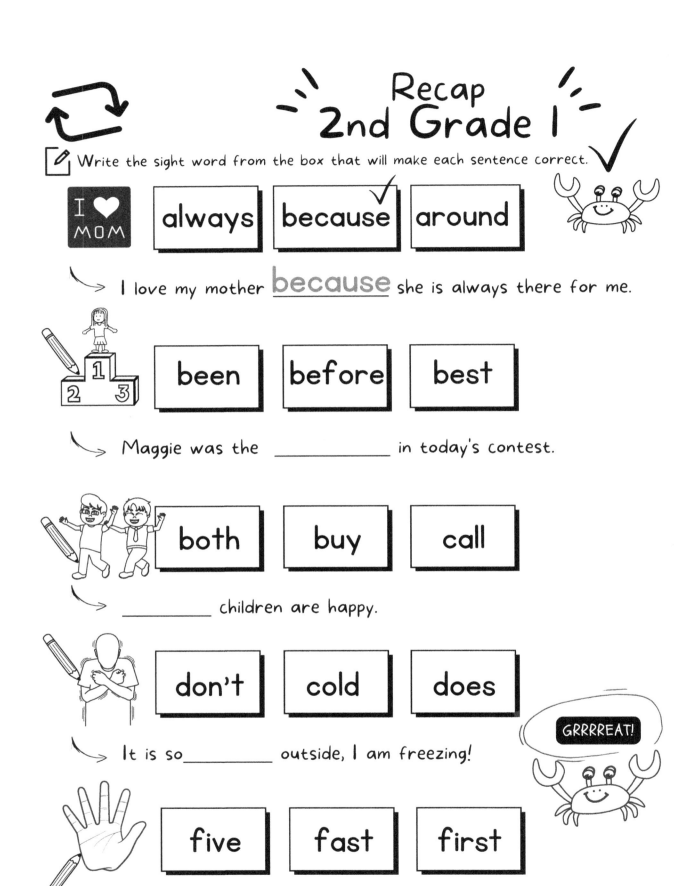

| always | because ✓ | around |

I love my mother __because__ she is always there for me.

| been | before | best |

Maggie was the _____ in today's contest.

| both | buy | call |

_____ children are happy.

| don't | cold | does |

It is so_____ outside, I am freezing!

GRRRREAT!

| five | fast | first |

We have _____ fingers on each hand.

Recap
2nd Grade I

After reading its meaning, write the corresponding sight word.

every time or
all the time → **always**

in a position or
direction surrounding

for the reason that

the number **5**

coming before all others
in order, time etc. **first**

moving or happening quickly,
able to move or happen quickly

at a low temperature, (way)
lower than body temperature

of the highest quality, or
being the most suitable, pleasing

In a sentence:

Mike found a $10 bill on the ground.

Sight Word #149. found

US / UK: /faʊnd/

Form a sentence with the given sight word.

_____

- -

_____

Meaning in English: past simple and past participle form of verb "to find".

In a sentence:

Phil gave me a small birthday gift.

Sight Word #150. gave

US / UK: /geɪv/

Form a sentence with the given sight word.

_____

- -

_____

Meaning in English: past simple form of verb "to give".

In a sentence:

What goes around comes around!

Sight Word #151. goes

US: /goʊz/
UK: /gəʊz/

Form a sentence with the given sight word.

_____

- -

_____

Meaning in English: he/she/it present simple form of verb "to go".

found   gave   goes

In a sentence:

What else is green besides the grass?

" —

👁 Sight
📢 Word #152. green

US / UK: /griːn/

💡 Form a sentence with the given sight word.

_____

- -

_____

📖 Meaning in English: of a colour between blue and yellow (adjective).

In a sentence:

The dog hurt its paw.

" —

👁 Sight
📢 Word #153. its

US / UK: /ɪts/

💡 Form a sentence with the given sight word.

_____

- -

_____

📖 Meaning in English: belonging to something that has already been mentioned (determiner).

In a sentence:

She made him cry for no reason.

" —

👁 Sight
📢 Word #154. made

US / UK: /meɪd/

💡 Form a sentence with the given sight word.

_____

- -

_____

📖 Meaning in English: past simple and past participle form of verb "to make".

✏️ green   its   made

In a sentence:

Many people bought tickets for the match.

Sight Word **#155. many**

US / UK: /ˈmen·i/

Form a sentence with the given sight word.

_____

- -

_____

Meaning in English: a large number / a lot (of) (adjective, pronoun).

In a sentence:

My father took **off** his hat.

Sight Word **#156. off**

US /ɑːf/
UK: /ɒf/

Form a sentence with the given sight word.

_____

- -

_____

Meaning in English: used with actions in which something is removed from a thing (adverb).

In a sentence:

Is it Monday **or** Tuesday today?

Sight Word **#157. or**

US: strong /ɔːr/ weak /ə/
UK: strong /ɔːr/ weak /ər/

Form a sentence with the given sight word.

_____

- -

_____

Meaning in English: used to connect different possibilities (conjunction).

many   off   or

In a sentence:

"— —
— — "

👁 Sight
📢 Word #158. pull

US / UK: /pʊl/

Don't pull the door, you need to push it!

💡 Form a sentence with the given sight word.

_____

- -

_____

📖 Meaning in English: to move something towards yourself (verb).

In a sentence:

"— —
— — "

👁 Sight
📢 Word #159. read

US / UK: /riːd/

She will read in front of everybody.

💡 Form a sentence with the given sight word.

_____

- -

_____

📖 Meaning in English: to obtain meaning or information by looking at written words (verb).

In a sentence:

"— —
— — "

👁 Sight
📢 Word #160. right

US / UK: /raɪt/

You got all the answers right.

💡 Form a sentence with the given sight word.

_____

- -

_____

📖 Meaning in English: suitable or correct, or as it should be (adjective).

✏️ pull   read   right

Write an original short story that contains the four sight words below. Tick them as you use them. ✓

many
green
found
or

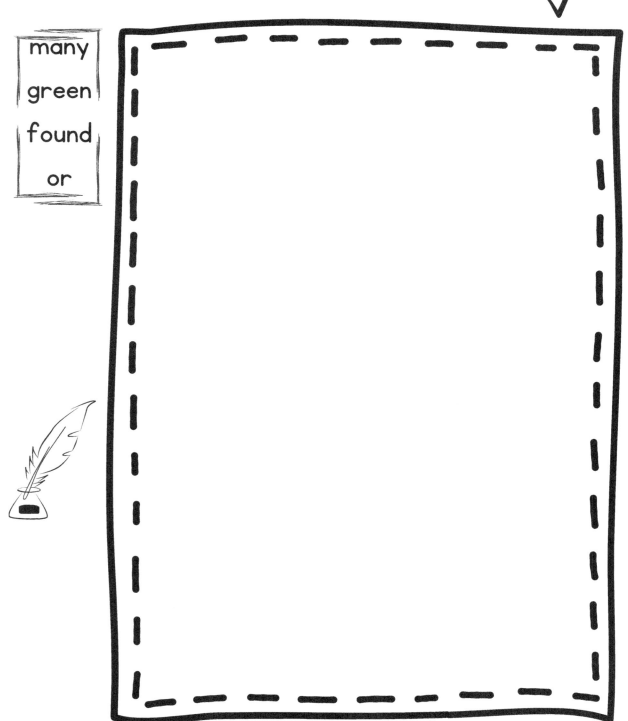

In a sentence:

My sister would like me to sing for her.

👁 Sight Word #161. sing

US / UK: /sɪŋ/

💡 Form a sentence with the given sight word.

_____

- -

_____

📖 Meaning in English: to make musical sounds with the voice (verb).

In a sentence:

Sit down, please! I will be right back.

👁 Sight Word #162. sit

US / UK: /sɪt/

💡 Form a sentence with the given sight word.

_____

- -

_____

📖 Meaning in English: to rest the lower part of the body on a seat (verb).

In a sentence:

I couldn't sleep well last night.

👁 Sight Word #163. sleep

US / UK: /sliːp/

💡 Form a sentence with the given sight word.

_____

- -

_____

📖 Meaning in English: to rest when your eyes are closed and your mind is unconscious (verb).

✏️ sing   sit   sleep

In a sentence:

Tell me about your holiday. How was it?

Sight Word #164. tell

US / UK: /tel/

Form a sentence with the given sight word.

_____

- -

_____

Meaning in English: to say something to someone, often giving them instructions (verb).

In a sentence:

He gave them their jackets.

Sight Word #165. their

US: /ðer/
UK: /ðeər/

Form a sentence with the given sight word.

_____

- -

_____

Meaning in English: belonging to or connected with them; possessive form of "they" (pronoun).

In a sentence:

What are these toys doing here?

Sight Word #166. these

US / UK: /ðiːz/

Form a sentence with the given sight word.

_____

- -

_____

Meaning in English: plural of "this" (determiner, pronoun).

tell   their   these

128

In a sentence:

Can I help you with those boxes?

Sight Word #167. those
US: /ðoʊz/
UK: /ðəʊz/

Form a sentence with the given sight word.

_____

- -

_____

Meaning in English: plural of "that" (determiner, pronoun).

In a sentence:

Upon her head she wore a black hat.

Sight Word #168. upon
US: /əˈpɑːn/
UK: /əˈpɒn/

Form a sentence with the given sight word.

_____

- -

_____

Meaning in English: on (preposition).

In a sentence:

Thank you for driving us to the station!

Sight Word #169. us
US / UK: /strong /ʌs/ weak /əs/

Form a sentence with the given sight word.

_____

- -

_____

Meaning in English: used to refer to a group that includes the speaker (pronoun).

those   upon   us

In a sentence:

Use scissors to cut the shapes out!

Sight Word #170. use

US / UK: /juːz/

Form a sentence with the given sight word.

_____

- -

_____

Meaning in English: to put something such as a tool, skill, or building to a purpose (verb).

In a sentence:

Thank you very much, I appreciate it!

Sight Word #171. very

US / UK: /ˈver.i/

Form a sentence with the given sight word.

_____

- -

_____

Meaning in English: to a great degree or extremely (adverb).

In a sentence:

We should wash our hands before we eat.

Sight Word #172. wash

US: /wɑːʃ/
UK: /wɒʃ/

Form a sentence with the given sight word.

_____

- -

_____

Meaning in English: to clean something using water (verb).

use   very   wash

In a sentence:

Which time suits you better?

👁 Sight Word

🔊

US / UK: /wɪtʃ/

#173. which

💡 Form a sentence with the given sight word.

_____

- -

_____

📖 Meaning in English: used in questions where there is a limited set of answers (determiner).

In a sentence:

Why do you like this workbook?

👁 Sight Word

🔊

US / UK: /waɪ/

#174. why

💡 Form a sentence with the given sight word.

_____

- -

_____

📖 Meaning in English: for what reason (adverb).

❗ Keep in mind.

Why __asks for an explanation__ or __reason for something.__

♡

Which __is the correct spelling__ of this sight word.

US / UK: /wɪtʃ/

#173. which

US / UK: /waɪ/

#174. why

❗

≠

witch

__Do not get confused.__ Even if "which" and "witch" sound identical, their meanings are very different.

131

In a sentence:

I wish I was a bit taller.

Sight Word #175. wish

US / UK: /wɪʃ/

Form a sentence with the given sight word.

Meaning in English: used with past simple to express that you feel sorry about a state (verb).

In a sentence:

Where does your father work?

Sight Word #176. work

US: /wɜ˞ːk/
UK: /wɜːk/

Form a sentence with the given sight word.

Meaning in English: to do a job, especially the job you do to earn money (verb).

In a sentence:

Would you rather be a bird or a fish?

Sight Word #177. would

US / UK: strong /wʊd/
weak /wəd/ /əd/

Form a sentence with the given sight word.

Meaning in English: used as a form of will in requests and offers (modal verb).

wish   work   would

In a sentence:

Please write the word in a sentence below!

👁 Sight Word

#178. write

US / UK: /raɪt/

💡 Form a sentence with the given sight word.

_____

- -

_____

📖 Meaning in English: to put letters, numbers on a piece of paper or a computer screen (verb).

In a sentence:

Is this your bicycle, Brenda?

👁 Sight Word

#179. your

US: strong /jʊr/ weak /jə/
UK: strong /jɔːr/ weak /jər/

💡 Form a sentence with the given sight word.

_____

- -

_____

📖 Meaning in English: belonging or relating to the person or being spoken to (determiner).

📝 <u>Write</u> the names of <u>your</u> trusted network, in each layer of the circle. The circle closest to you, would be those that you trust the most.

US / UK: /raɪt/

#178. write

US: strong /jʊr/ weak /jə/
UK: strong /jɔːr/ weak /jər/

#179. your

ME

For example, the closest circle may be your parents, and the furthest circle is a TV star. You can write more than one safety person in each layer.

133

Write the sight words in this chapter in alphabetical order.

always around because

Recap
2nd Grade 3

Use each given sight word in a sentence.

green

its

made

pull

read

right

would

write

your

Use each given sight word in a sentence.

been

best

both

buy

call

cold

five

gave

sing

- There are _____ 2nd Grade sight words;
- The sight word that you like the most (in this chapter) is _____ .
- There are ____ six-letter sight words in this chapter.
- There are ____ five-letter sight words in this chapter.
- There are ____ four-letter sight words in this chapter.

CHAPTER 3

YOU'VE MADE IT ONCE AGAIN! YOU ARE EXTRAORDINARY!

- The 13th sight word in this chapter is: _____;
- The 22nd sight word in this chapter is: _____;
- The 7 "w" words in this chapter are:

wash   which   why

__sh   _o__   w___d

____e

In a sentence:

What is the book about?

Sight Word #180. about

US / UK: /əˈbaʊt/

Form a sentence with the given sight word.

Meaning in English: on the subject of, or connected with (preposition).

In a sentence:

The book was better than I expected.

Sight Word #181. better

US: /ˈbet̬.ɚ/
UK: /ˈbet̬.ər/

Form a sentence with the given sight word.

Meaning in English: comparative of "good" - of a higher standard, or more suitable, pleasing, or effective than other things or people (adjective).

In a sentence:

They always bring their cat with them.

Sight Word #182. bring

US / UK: /brɪŋ/

Form a sentence with the given sight word.

Meaning in English: to take or carry someone or something to a place or a person, or in the direction of the person speaking (verb).

about   better   bring

Sight Word #183. carry

US: /ˈker.i/
UK: /ˈkær.i/

In a sentence:
Would you like me to carry your bag for you?

💡 Form a sentence with the given sight word.

_____

- -

_____

📖 Meaning in English: to hold something or someone with your hands, arms, or on your back and transport it, him, or her from one place to another (verb).

Sight Word #184. clean

US / UK: /kliːn/

In a sentence:
We always make sure our hands are clean before we eat.

💡 Form a sentence with the given sight word.

_____

- -

_____

📖 Meaning in English: free from any dirty marks, pollution, bacteria, etc. (adjective).

Sight Word #185. cut

US / UK: /kʌt/

In a sentence:
I asked mom to cut a slice of bread for me as I was having breakfast.

💡 Form a sentence with the given sight word.

_____

- -

_____

📖 Meaning in English: to break the surface of something, or to divide or make something smaller, using a sharp tool, especially a knife (verb).

carry   clean   cut

In a sentence:
Are you done with those scissors yet?

Sight Word #186. done

US / UK: /dʌn/

💡 Form a sentence with the given sight word.

_____

- -

_____

Meaning in English: If something is done, or you are done with it, it is finished, or you have finished doing, using it, etc. (adjective).

💡 Describe crabs by writing a sentence or drawing a picture in each box.

✏️ What are they?

✏️ Where do they live?

✏️ What do they eat?

Are you done?

Done

140

Sight Word #187. draw

US: /drɑː/
UK: /drɔː/

In a sentence:

"Please draw a purple line at the bottom of the page", teacher said.

Form a sentence with the given sight word.

Meaning in English: to make a picture of something or someone with a pencil or pen (verb).

Sight Word #188. drink

US / UK: /drɪŋk/

In a sentence:

I normally drink a lot of water after an intense training session.

Form a sentence with the given sight word.

Meaning in English: to take liquid into the body through the mouth (verb).

Sight Word #189. eight

US / UK: /eɪt/

In a sentence:

He was eight (years old) when his family moved here.

Form a sentence with the given sight word.

Meaning in English: the number 8.

draw   drink   eight

In a sentence:

"The path is steep, so be careful that you do not fall", the guide said.

Sight Word #190. fall

US: /fɑːl/
UK: /fɔːl/

Form a sentence with the given sight word.

_____

_ _

_____

Meaning in English: to suddenly go down onto the ground or towards the ground without intending to or by accident (verb).

In a sentence:

How far is it from Australia to New Zealand?

Sight Word #191. far

US: /fɑːr/
UK: /fɑːr/

Form a sentence with the given sight word.

_____

_ _

_____

Meaning in English: at, to, or from a great distance in space or time (adverb).

In a sentence:

"This jar is very full so be careful with it", grandma said.

Sight Word #192. full

US / UK: /fʊl/

Form a sentence with the given sight word.

_____

_ _

_____

Meaning in English: (of a container or a space) holding or containing as much as possible or a lot (adjective).

fall   far   full

142

After reading its meaning, write the corresponding sight word.

at, to, or from a great
distance in space or time

to take liquid into the
body through the mouth

free from any dirty marks,
pollution, bacteria, etc.

the number **8**

on the subject of,
or connected with

comparative
of "good"

holding or containing as
much as possible or a lot

to suddenly go down
onto the ground

In a sentence:

I got an apple in my hand, I will eat it soon.

Sight Word #193. got

US: /gɑːt/
UK: /gɒt/

Form a sentence with the given sight word.

_____

- -

_____

Meaning in English: past simple and past participle form of verb "to get".

In a sentence:

It is unbelievable how quickly children grow!

Sight Word #194. grow

US: /groʊ/
UK: /grəʊ/

Form a sentence with the given sight word.

_____

- -

_____

Meaning in English: to increase in size or amount, or to become more advanced or developed (verb).

In a sentence:

"Please hold this bag while I open the door", the taxi driver said.

Sight Word #195. hold

US: /hoʊld/
UK: /həʊld/

Form a sentence with the given sight word.

_____

- -

_____

Meaning in English: to take and keep something in your hand or arms (verb).

got   grow   hold

Sight Word #196. hot

US: /hɑːt/
UK: /hɒt/

In a sentence:

It's too hot in here, can we turn down the heating?

Form a sentence with the given sight word.

_____

Meaning in English: having a high temperature (adjective).

Sight Word #197. hurt

US: /hɜ˞ːt/
UK: /hɜːt/

In a sentence:

"Does it hurt?", the doctor asked. "No, it does not hurt", I replied.

Form a sentence with the given sight word.

_____

Meaning in English: to feel pain in a part of your body, or to injure someone or cause them pain (verb).

Sight Word #198. if

US / UK: /ɪf/

In a sentence:

Please tell me if you need any help with that activity.

Form a sentence with the given sight word.

_____

Meaning in English: used when you want to make a polite offer, request, or remark (conjunction).

hot   hurt   if

In a sentence:

Do you want this photograph back or can I keep it?

Sight Word #199. keep

US / UK: /kiːp/

💡 Form a sentence with the given sight word.

_____

- -

_____

🔍 Meaning in English: to have or continue to have in your possession (verb).

In a sentence:

Kimberly is such a very kind and thoughtful person.

Sight Word #200. kind

US / UK: /kaɪnd/

💡 Form a sentence with the given sight word.

_____

- -

_____

🔍 Meaning in English: generous, helpful, and thinking about other people's feelings (adjective).

In a sentence:

My father is really, really funny. He always makes me laugh!

Sight Word #201. laugh

US: /læf/
UK: /lɑːf/

💡 Form a sentence with the given sight word.

_____

- -

_____

🔍 Meaning in English: to smile while making sounds with your voice that show you think something is funny or you are happy (verb).

keep   kind   laugh

Sight Word #202. light

US / UK: /laɪt/

In a sentence:
The traffic was quite light so we got through Manchester quickly.

Form a sentence with the given sight word.

_____

- -

_____

Meaning in English: not great in strength or amount (adjective).

Sight Word #203. long

US: /lɑːŋ/
UK: /lɒŋ/

In a sentence:
There was a long queue at the post office.

Form a sentence with the given sight word.

_____

- -

_____

Meaning in English: being a distance between two points that is more than average or usual, or being of a particular length (adjective).

Sight Word #204. much

US / UK: /mʌtʃ/

In a sentence:
Children never eat much, but they seem healthy.

Form a sentence with the given sight word.

_____

- -

_____

Meaning in English: a large amount or to a large degree (determiner).

light   long   much

Sight Word #205. myself

US / UK: /maɪˈself/

In a sentence:
So I thought to myself: it's time to take a well-deserved nap.

Form a sentence with the given sight word.

_____

_____

Meaning in English: used when the subject of the verb is "I" and the object is the same person (pronoun).

Sight Word #206. never

US: /ˈnev.ɚ/
UK: /ˈnev.ər/

In a sentence:
I have never been to Australia. Have you ever been there?

Form a sentence with the given sight word.

_____

_____

Meaning in English: not at any time or not on any occasion (adverb).

Sight Word #207. only

US: /ˈoʊn.li/
UK: /ˈəʊn.li/

In a sentence:
Mandy was the only person remaining in the classroom during the break.

Form a sentence with the given sight word.

_____

_____

Meaning in English: used to show that there is a single one or very few of something, or that there are no others (adjective).

myself   never   only

Write the sight word from the box that will make each sentence correct.

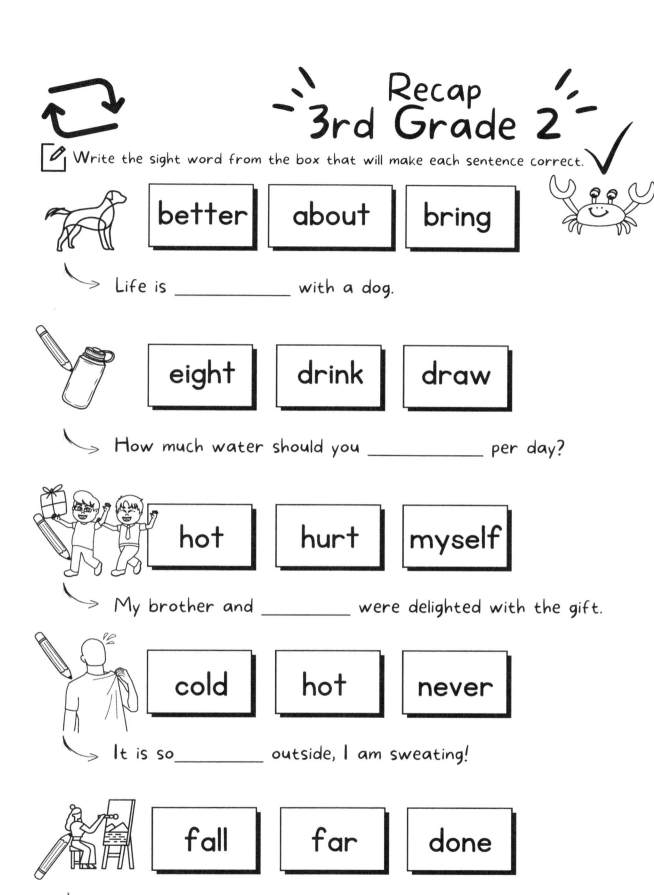

| better | about | bring |

Life is _____ with a dog.

| eight | drink | draw |

How much water should you _____ per day?

| hot | hurt | myself |

My brother and _____ were delighted with the gift.

| cold | hot | never |

It is so_____ outside, I am sweating!

| fall | far | done |

The painting is almost _____.

149

In a sentence:

Each neighborhood in New Jersey has its own characteristics.

Sight Word

#208. own

US: /oʊn/
UK: /əʊn/

Form a sentence with the given sight word.

_____

- -

_____

Meaning in English: belonging to or done by a particular person or thing (determiner, pronoun).

In a sentence:

Pick a card from the pack, then pass the pack to the next person.

Sight Word

#209. pick

US / UK: /pɪk/

Form a sentence with the given sight word.

_____

- -

_____

Meaning in English: to take some things and leave others (verb).

In a sentence:

The restaurant is open seven days a week.

Sight Word

#210. seven

US / UK: /ˈsev.ən/

Form a sentence with the given sight word.

_____

- -

_____

Meaning in English: the number 7.

own   pick   seven

In a sentence:
Shall we go in the playground?

Sight Word
#211. shall
US / UK: strong /ʃæl/ weak /ʃəl/

Form a sentence with the given sight word.

_____

- -

_____

Meaning in English: used, with "I" or "we", to make a suggestion (modal verb).

In a sentence:
Let me show you this new book I've just bought.

Sight Word
#212. show
US: /ʃoʊ/
US: /ʃəʊ/

Form a sentence with the given sight word.

_____

- -

_____

Meaning in English: to make it possible for something to be seen (verb).

In a sentence:
The other restaurant is open only six days a week.

Sight Word
#213. six
US / UK: /'sɪks/

Form a sentence with the given sight word.

_____

- -

_____

Meaning in English: the number 6.

shall   show   six

In a sentence:

That T-shirt is too small for you.

Sight Word

US / UK: /smaːl/

#214. small

Form a sentence with the given sight word.

_____

- -

_____

Meaning in English: little in size or amount when compared with what is typical or average (adjective).

In a sentence:

When do you start your new job?

Sight Word

US: /staːrt/
US: /staːt/

#215. start

Form a sentence with the given sight word.

_____

- -

_____

Meaning in English: to begin doing something (verb).

In a sentence:

We can take ten (people) in the minibus.

Sight Word

US / UK: /ten/

#216. ten

Form a sentence with the given sight word.

_____

- -

_____

Meaning in English: the number 10.

small   start   ten

In a sentence:

Today is even hotter than yesterday, isn't it?

Sight Word #217. today

US / UK: /tə'deɪ/

Form a sentence with the given sight word.

Meaning in English: (on) the present day (adverb, noun).

Draw on the face how you feel today and complete the sentences below. You can only use the words "good" and great.

Today

I feel

Tomorrow will be

a _____ day.

In a sentence:
We used to go skiing together.

Sight Word

#218. together
US: /təˈɡeð.ɚ/
UK: /təˈɡeð.ər/

Form a sentence with the given sight word.

_____

- -

_____

Meaning in English: with each other (adverb).

In a sentence:
I'll try to give her a call again tomorrow morning.

Sight Word

#219. try
US / UK: /traɪ/

Form a sentence with the given sight word.

_____

- -

_____

Meaning in English: to attempt to do something (verb).

In a sentence:
I put my hands in my pockets to keep them warm.

Sight Word

#220. warm
US / UK: /wɔːrm/

Form a sentence with the given sight word.

_____

- -

_____

Meaning in English: having or producing a comfortably high temperature, although not hot (adjective).

together   try   warm

✏️ Write the sight words in this chapter in alphabetical order.

about better bring

Recap
3rd Grade 3

✎ Use each given sight word in a sentence.

about

cut

clean

drink

far

full

got

grow

hold

Recap
3rd Grade 3

✏️ Use each given sight word in a sentence.

hot

myself

never

shall

small

start

today

try

warm

Chapter Summary
3rd Grade

- There are _____ 3rd Grade sight words;
- The sight word that you like the most (in this chapter) is _____ .
- There are ____ six-letter sight words in this chapter.
- There are ____ five-letter sight words in this chapter.
- There are ____ four-letter sight words in this chapter.

CHAPTER 3

YOU'VE MADE IT ONCE AGAIN! YOU ARE EXTRAORDINARY!

- The 17th sight word in this chapter is: _____;
- The 2nd sight word in this chapter is: _____;
- The 5 "s" words in this chapter are:

S_____   S____   S__

S_____   S_____

Thank You

As a small family business, your feedback is very important to us and we would really appreciate if you could take a little time to rate it on Amazon.
This would be very useful not only for us - the creators of this educational resource - but also for other people looking for a workbook like this.

We really hope you enjoy our work and find it extremely useful for your child(ren).

We create our books with lots of love, still mistakes can always happen. Therefore, if there are any issues with your book such as printing errors or faulty bindings, please contact the platform you purchased it from to obtain a replacement.

For any other suggestions and/or remarks, do not forget to contact us at:

contact@smartdevpress.com

SMARTDEV PRESS

More from our SIGHT WORDS Workbooks for KIDS

Vol. 2

COMMON NOUNS

95 MUST KNOW COMMON NOUNS

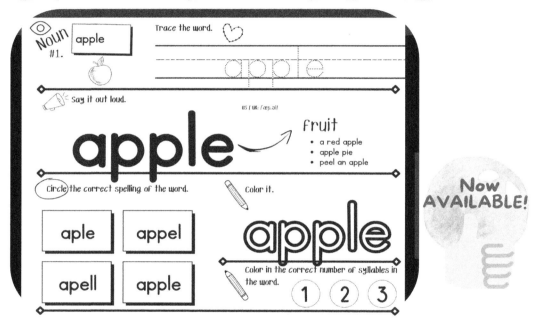

220 Words. Plus 95 Nouns. The Logical Continuation.
Pre-primer. Primer. First. Second. Third.

Now AVAILABLE!
